THE INCREDIBLE SPICE MEN

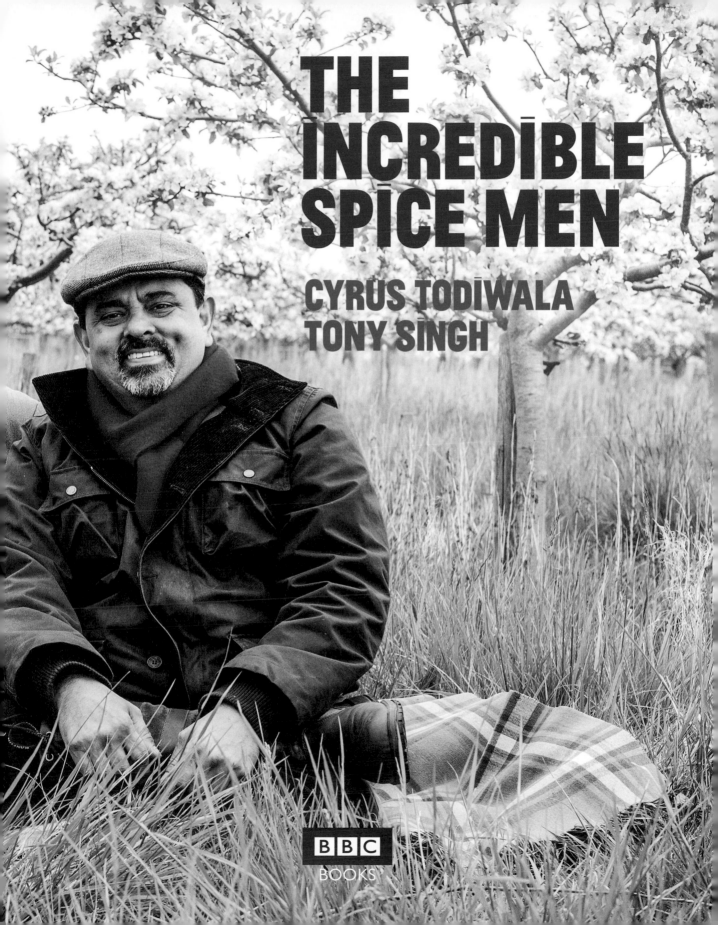

THE INCREDIBLE SPICE MEN

CYRUS TODIWALA
TONY SINGH

BBC BOOKS

CONTENTS

INTRODUCTION
CYRUS TODIWALA

Tony and I have been friends for quite a time now, but we come from different sides of the world, and from different religious and social cultures. Tony is a Sikh and a fourth generation Scot, born in Scotland. I am a Parsee and Zoroastrian, born in Bombay, but England has been my home since I moved here over twenty years ago.

At the same time, though, Tony and I share much more than divides us: we are passionately British, although still very much tied to the subcontinent, and we are equally passionate about cooking, eating and spicing. Spices are in our blood, so it was almost inevitable that we should join in a quest to reintroduce Britain to the magic that is spices. Together we have become spice missionaries, and we hope very sincerely that we can convert you.

I grew up with spices; in India everyone does. My mother was a great cook, for a start – everything we ate was imbued with spices and flavour – and she was also a good teacher. Most of what I know today about cooking and cuisine started in my mother's kitchen. When I reached the age of responsibility – perhaps around seven? – I was sent to buy what we needed for the day's meals, animal, vegetable and spice. By this time, I knew what to look for in a spice: for example, the right colour of cardamom pod and peppercorns that hadn't been adulterated with dried papaya seeds. The stallholders would be scathing: 'Go away, child,' as I carefully watched their scale for an errant finger weighting it down. (Spices at that time were sold in 10g portions, so the scales were goldsmiths' scales, tiny, easy to unbalance.) Later I earned some pocket money by doing the shopping for all of our neighbours. I would spend my earnings on fruit trifle, basically jelly and custard – I've always had a sweet tooth!

But the fact is, I knew my spices, and even now, everything to do with spices fascinates me. Spices are, variously and magically, the seeds, bark, buds, kernels, berries, pods, fruits and rhizomes of various trees, shrubs, vines and grasses. Most of the important spice plants come from tropical Asia: these include cassia, cardamom, cinnamon, pepper, star anise and cloves. Several spices, such as cumin, coriander, caraway, dill and fennel, originate from nearer home, from Europe and western Asia.

And it was only in the sixteenth century that many spices from the Americas were introduced to Europe and the wider world, including such widespread flavours as allspice and vanilla.

Spices have been used since time immemorial, not only in cooking but also for medicinal purposes. For instance, cassia and cinnamon are both mentioned in Chinese herbals dating back some 4,500 years. Ayurvedic medicine in India has always valued spices, and in both China and India, spices are still used in cooking as much for their perceived ability to promote health as for the wondrous flavours they impart to food.

During the fifteenth and sixteenth centuries in Europe, spices were very highly valued, and unbelievably expensive to buy. They were thought to be so protective against illness, including the dreaded plague, that many were willing to risk their lives in pursuit of them. It was the European appetite for spices, particularly for cloves, cinnamon and nutmeg, that was the driving force behind that era's great and dangerous voyages of discovery: Columbus, for instance, only discovered the Americas because he was seeking an alternative, westerly route to the East and its wealth of spices.

Spices were always an important item of trade. The Chinese took them along the Silk Road, the Arabs introduced them to Europe. But there was a dark heart to the spice trade. While fortunes were made, many lives were lost in the greedy pursuit of spices. However, control over the pepper trade, for instance, was one of the factors that led to the British Raj, to Anglo-Indian cuisine, to the spread of curry restaurants – and thus spices – throughout Britain from the 1920s.

It seems to me that Britain today has forgotten about spices to a large extent. Tony and I want to jog your memories, to get you to dust off old habits, to bring your spice jars from the back of the cupboard to the front (you can even keep them in your fridge – it will preserve the spices for much longer). We want you to re-think how and what you cook, every time you cook. In Britain we have some of the best meats and fish in the world, and a multitude of wonderful home-grown and imported fruit and vegetables. We also have access to some of the best spices in the world. Whenever I go back to India, I have to take spices with me, as the best Indian spices are actually exported to the UK!

Learn how to spice up your basic recipes – a pinch here and there – and don't be afraid. 'Spicy' doesn't necessarily mean 'hot': spices are also sweet, warm and pungent, and will add colour, drama and excitement to your everyday cooking. And we mean *every* day...

Tony and I share a simple message: let's spice up Britain again!

INTRODUCTION TONY SINGH

Over the years of knowing Cyrus, I've absorbed a lot of Todiwala knowledge and philosophy and, although from different countries, essentially we're coming from the same place. We love cooking, food, British ingredients and spices – already a good enough basis for friendship! It's also a good excuse for us to get together, in the television programmes and in this book, to sell our concept of spicing to the Great British public. Cyrus thinks of us as missionaries, aiming for conversion. I think I'm more like a soldier preparing for battle...

For I am a Sikh, and the Sikhs are great warriors. I am a Sikh born in Scotland, and I am very proud to be both Scottish and Sikh. The Sikhism I inherited from my grandparents and parents has played a major part in defining who and what I am. Its central belief is equality between all people and this is regardless of religion, caste, colour, creed, age, gender or social status. (This was a really revolutionary idea in the caste-dominated society of India in the sixteenth century, when Sikhism began.) A cornerstone of Sikhism is the *langar*, or community kitchen, and preparing food, cooking food, helping to serve it and, yes, washing up, were all part of my life from the very earliest days. I was always hungry as a lad, so I soon learned that if I helped my aunties I would get extra goodies to eat – as well as a pat on the head! I later took a Home Economics class at school: I was quite attracted to the idea of cooking as a career by then but, to be honest, I mainly saw it as a skivers' class, like drama. However I won an HE prize, which I didn't tell anyone about for a while: that wasn't what boys (or men) did in Scotland then!

And I can't deny the influence both my parents had on me as well. Mum, like Cyrus's mum, was a very good cook. She cooked traditional Punjabi food, which was quite difficult in Scotland because there was nothing in the way of ingredients, but as she'd had British-based domestic science classes at school too, she was able to cook Scottish treats for us – things like drop scones and shortbread (sometimes spiced). She was able to take elements from both cultures – she cooks a mean haggis pakora – and I have to admit that she's probably well ahead in the spice race that Cyrus and I have entered! Dad's input was no less significant. He had probably hoped to hand on

his business – a corner shop – to his sons, but at the same time, very generously, he thought it important for us to follow our dreams. As a result, my brother joined the RAF, my younger brother went into window cleaning and I became a chef.

It was difficult at first. I was classically trained at college in Edinburgh, so kept away from the spices I had been brought up with. However, perhaps not surprisingly, as soon as possible employers saw me, they said, 'We don't do curry, son.' I had to fight extra hard – nobody was used to a chef with a turban – but gradually I got some really good jobs, amongst them the Royal Scotsman and the Royal Yacht Britannia (strictly no spices). Then, funnily enough, I remembered what I should never have forgotten, that spices actually enhance food, that they do just make food taste better.

The Great British public, too, seems to have forgotten about spices, although the country has a long history of spice use. The Romans, for instance, introduced many herbs and spices when they were here, over 2,000 years ago. In the Middle Ages, the Crusaders brought back spices that they had encountered in the Middle East. At around that time, British food became very highly spiced indeed, possibly to cover up the taste of salt (most meats and vegetables would have been salt-preserved) or tainted meat. The spice then seemed to go out of British life, possibly because of Puritanism – plain is best – although many think that the rigours of two world wars, and food rationing, had a lasting effect on the way the British cook.

There are still sneaky reminders of Britain's spicy past, though, in many historic British dishes – the cayenne sprinkled on top of fried whitebait, the devilled sauces for kidneys, mushrooms and eggs, the ginger in gingerbread and parkin, the cinnamon in mince pies, the nutmeg in custards, and the ubiquitous clove in apple pies. It is obvious that British cooking throughout the centuries has absorbed lots of influences, including spices, and I think it can learn to do so again. For a start, ask anyone what the best-known British dishes are, and I bet they list roast beef, fish and chips and – yes – chicken tikka masala! It's said to have been invented in Britain, when a restaurant customer looked at their dry plate of chicken tikka, and asked 'Where's the gravy?' A quick heating through of tinned tomato soup plus a few spices (the masala), and a new Great British classic was allegedly born.

Britain has some of the best produce in the world – meat, fish, cheese, cider and (one of my personal favourites) whisky. I think such good produce, although great on its own, can be made even tastier with the addition of spice. You'll see, throughout the recipes in the book, how we have committed what looks like culinary treason on many of the most revered and traditional of British dishes. All I can say is, give it a try, see how you like it. To paraphrase Julius Caesar, another incoming soldier on a mission, 'We came, we saw and (we hope) spices have conquered.'

STARTERS,
SNACKS
& A LIGHT BITE OR TWO

Is it any wonder that most people hate beetroots when we completely waste them by boiling them up or serving them in vinegar? This is a great soup that I make all the time, and I always love seeing people's reactions when I serve it to them. They usually wince at the sight of beetroot, but don't say anything out of politeness, then are completely won over with the first sip. I've served this at some very snooty dinners and it has never let me down.

Cyrus's
SPĪCED BEETROOT SOUP

1 Wash the lentils well. If using yellow lentils, soak for 3 hours then drain. To a large pan add the prepared lentils, the beetroot and the boiling water. Bring to a boil and then reduce the heat, partly cover with a lid and simmer, stirring occasionally, for 45 minutes–1¼ hours, until the beetroot and lentils are tender. Add a little more boiling water if the mixture starts to look dry, but don't add too much as you don't want a watery soup.

2 Blend the mixture to a smooth purée, then strain through a fine sieve. Return the purée to a clean pan and stir in the coconut milk and salt. If necessary, add a little more boiling water to thin the soup, but it should be quite thick and velvety. Keep warm over a low heat.

3 To prepare the spices, heat the oil in a frying pan over a medium-high heat and have a lid handy. When the oil starts to just smoke add the mustard seeds, cover the pan (the seeds fly all over the place as they crackle and pop) and turn the heat down. After 10–15 seconds add the cumin and the curry leaves and fry for 1 minute.

4 Tip the contents of the frying pan, including any oil, into the soup and stir well. Taste, add salt if necessary, and dilute with hot water or a little more coconut milk if you prefer a lighter soup. Stir in the fresh coriander and serve in bowls, drizzled with a swirl of double cream if you like.

SERVES 4

FOR THE SOUP
100g (4oz) split orange or yellow lentils
400g (14oz) beetroot, peeled and cut into 2cm (¾in) chunks
1 litre (1¾ pints) boiling water
180ml (6fl oz) tinned coconut milk, plus extra to taste
½–1 tsp salt, or to taste

FOR THE SPICES
2 tbsp rapeseed oil, vegetable oil or other clear cooking oil
2 tsp black mustard seeds
1 tsp cumin seeds, gently crushed
a good handful of finely shredded curry leaves (optional)
2 tbsp chopped fresh coriander leaves
double cream, to drizzle (optional)

I was waiting for staff lunch at my restaurant once when someone slipped a hot, steaming bowl of this wonderful soup – aromatic, pungent and spicy – under my nose. But before I could tuck in, they slipped some deep-fried fish heads into the bowl too! A bit of a shocker, but once I tried it the taste was brilliant, and the texture of the fish complemented the soup perfectly. I've refined it a little, as most people would get a fright at the sight of fish heads bobbing about in their soup!

Tony's

HOT & SOUR SOUP WITH CRISPY FISH

1 Mix all of the marinade ingredients together in a shallow bowl that will hold all the fish. Add the fish, stir well to coat and leave to marinate for at least 15 minutes.

2 To prepare the soup, heat the sesame oil in a large saucepan and fry the ginger, garlic and red chilli over a low heat to soften. After a few minutes add the onion, baby corn, red or yellow pepper and carrot and fry for a further 4–5 minutes. Add the stock, then stir in the two soy sauces, the Worcestershire sauce and the vinegar, and bring to the boil.

3 In a small bowl, mix together the teaspoon of cornflour and 2 teaspoons of water. Stir this mixture into the boiling soup and continue boiling for a few minutes to thicken. Once thickened, add a splash of water if you feel the soup is too thick, and adjust the seasoning to taste. Keep warm over a low heat.

4 To cook the fish, in a large heavy-based pan heat enough oil to come roughly two-thirds up the sides of the pan. You can check that the oil is at the correct temperature by dropping a cube of bread into the hot oil; it should become golden-brown and crisp within a minute.

5 Sprinkle the cornflour onto a shallow plate and coat the marinated fish all over with it. Carefully drop the fish pieces into the hot oil and fry for 2–3 minutes until golden brown. Remove with a slotted spoon and drain on a plate lined with kitchen paper.

6 Transfer the hot soup to a serving dish or individual bowls, and top with crispy fish. Sprinkle with spring onions and serve.

SERVES 4

400g (14oz) firm-fleshed fish, such as cod, skin on, chopped into bite-sized pieces
rapeseed oil or vegetable oil, for deep-frying
50g (2oz) cornflour
6 spring onions, chopped, to serve

FOR THE MARINADE

1 tbsp light soy sauce
1 heaped tsp pickled ginger, chopped
½ tsp ground Sichuan pepper
1 tsp chilli flakes

FOR THE SOUP

3 tbsp sesame oil
2cm (1in) piece of fresh root ginger, chopped
3 garlic cloves, chopped
½ red chilli, seeds removed if liked, chopped
½ red onion, sliced
8 cobs baby corn (90g/3½oz), sliced lengthways
½ red or yellow pepper, sliced
1 carrot, sliced
1.5 litres (2½ pints) fish stock, or chicken stock
1 tbsp light soy sauce
1 tbsp dark soy sauce
1 tbsp Worcestershire sauce
2 tbsp white wine vinegar
1 tsp cornflour
salt

Gazpacho, the chilled Spanish soup, is a classic – but we are here to push a few boundaries, and to encourage you to alter a few bits here and there to create your very own specialities. In summer, when good British tomatoes are in season, the sun is blazing, the barbecue is lit and friends arrive, a good well-chilled gazpacho will make the world go round. The preparations can seem daunting, but believe you me, as long as you have a good blender you will complete the job in a jiffy.

Cyrus's

GAZPACHO WITH A KICK

SERVES 4-6

1 small cucumber or half a large one
1kg (2lb 4oz) ripe tomatoes,
    roughly chopped
1 green pepper, seeds removed,
    chopped
2-3 spring onions, white part only,
    chopped (reserve green parts
    for the garnish)
1 small red onion, chopped
2 garlic cloves, roughly chopped
1 mild green chilli, seeds removed,
    chopped
a large handful of basil leaves
a handful of coriander leaves and
    tender stems
1-1½ tbsp sherry vinegar (or use
    sherry and a dash of other vinegar)
75-100ml (2½-3½fl oz) extra-virgin
    olive oil

FOR THE SEASONING

1 tsp cumin seeds, very finely ground
½ tsp crushed black peppercorns
a few drops Tabasco (optional)
1 tsp salt, then more as desired

FOR THE CHILLI CROÛTONS

1 small baguette or half a large one,
    cut into roughly 20-25 thin slices
    (stale bread works well)
2 tbsp butter, softened
1 garlic clove, finely crushed
½ tsp chilli powder

FOR THE GARNISH

reserved spring onion green parts,
    thinly sliced
reserved cucumber skins, drained
    and finely chopped
½ small red onion, very finely
    chopped
½ red pepper, seeds removed,
    finely chopped
1 tbsp chopped fresh coriander leaves
a few basil leaves, torn
ice cubes

1 Peel the cucumber and reserve the skin. Place the skin in a bowl of cold water and set aside for the garnish. Chop the flesh roughly. Place all the soup ingredients, except the reserved cucumber skin, vinegar and olive oil, into a blender and blend until smooth.

2 Add 1 tbsp of the vinegar and 75ml (2½fl oz) of the oil and blend, then taste and add more oil and vinegar if liked. Strain through a coarse sieve over a bowl and press through as much as you can, squeezing out all liquid with a spatula or the back of a large wooden spoon.

3 Stir all of the seasoning ingredients into the strained soup. Adjust the seasoning to taste, then cover and chill until needed.

4 To make the chilli croûtons, preheat the oven to 160°C/325°F/gas 3. Arrange the slices of bread evenly in single layers on baking sheets. Cook in the preheated oven for 5 minutes, then turn the slices over and cook for a further 5 minutes or until crisp and lightly golden. Remove to cool slightly but do not turn the oven off.

5 Mix the butter with the garlic and chilli powder. Just before serving, spread a little chilli butter on all the toasted bread slices. Reduce the oven temperature to minimum and return the toasts to the oven to warm through and keep warm until ready to serve.

6 Gently mix together all of the garnish ingredients except the ice cubes. To serve, portion the soup out into cups or bowls and place an ice cube or two in each. Spoon a little garnish onto each soup, and serve with the chilli croûtons on the side.

This is one of the simplest, sexiest, most luxurious vegetable dishes you can get, with a wee twist of lime, coriander and a touch of chilli. Also, we couldn't resist sharing another favourite of ours as an option for you: saffron aioli made with rapeseed oil. It's another winner, smooth and creamy but with a warming saffron flavour. Choose which sauce you prefer, or ring the changes and make a different one each time.

Tony's

ASPARAGUS WITH LIME & CORIANDER HOLLANDAISE

1 Put all ingredients for the hollandaise reduction into a small stainless steel or ceramic-lined pan (do not use copper, cast-iron or aluminium, which tend to react with acidic foods). Bring to the boil and boil for 3-4 minutes to reduce the liquid to just 2 tsp of liquor; take care, it will evaporate quickly. Strain the liquor through a sieve and leave to cool.

2 For the hollandaise sauce, gently melt the clarified butter and keep warm. Put the egg yolks and half of the vinegar reduction in a small heatproof bowl. (Reserve the remaining vinegar for another time; it will keep in the fridge for a week.) Set this bowl over a pan of barely simmering water, checking that the water does not touch the base of the bowl, and whisk with a hand-held electric whisk until the mixture begins to thicken. Switch off the heat and remove the bowl from pan.

3 Continue to whisk while slowly trickling in the warm clarified butter; the sauce will thicken. Add a pinch of chilli powder, a squeeze of fresh lime juice, and salt to taste. Mix in the chopped herbs and place the bowl back over the pan of water to keep warm, without turning the heat back on.

4 Bring a large pan of salted water to the boil. Drop in the asparagus and simmer for 3-5 minutes until just tender. Drain and serve with the spiced hollandaise sauce on top and a wedge of lime on the side.

NOTE: For the saffron aioli, toast the saffron in a dry pan for 1 minute, then set aside in a bowl with the lemon juice and Pernod Ricard. Bring a pan of water to the boil and add the whole egg and 4 of the garlic cloves. Boil for 8-10 minutes, then remove. Peel the hard-boiled egg and set aside the white (keep it to put in a sandwich). Allow the yolk and the garlic to cool. Put all 5 garlic cloves, the mustard, all 3 egg yolks, the saffron mixture and seasoning in a food processor. Pour the oil into the running processor in a slow, steady stream, until it forms a thick sauce.

SERVES 4–6
1kg (2lb 4oz) asparagus, washed and ends snapped off (about 8 spears per person)
salt

FOR THE HOLLANDAISE REDUCTION
20ml (¾fl oz) white wine vinegar
juice of 1 lime
40ml (1¾fl oz) water
1 small shallot, chopped
30 coriander seeds
1 tsp black peppercorns
sprig of coriander
sprig of tarragon
1 bay leaf

FOR THE HOLLANDAISE SAUCE
150g (5oz) unsalted clarified butter (ghee)
2 egg yolks
a pinch of chilli powder
juice of about ½ lime, plus wedges to serve
2 tbsp chopped fresh coriander
1 tbsp chopped fresh tarragon
salt

FOR THE SAFFRON AIOLI (OPTIONAL)
½ tsp saffron strands
juice of 1 lemon
1 tbsp Pernod Ricard
1 egg, plus 2 yolks
5 cloves garlic, peeled
½ tsp Dijon mustard
250ml (9fl oz) rapeseed oil

Drop scones – a Scottish tradition, and these ones are based on my mum's recipe. We wanted to try a healthier, more substantial version of the classic drop scone, so we've roasted and puréed a butternut squash and added it to the batter, and spiced it up with some cinnamon. We thought the result was fantastic, and we hope you enjoy them.

Tony's
WARM BUTTERNUT SCONES WITH CHEESE

1 Preheat the oven to 180°C/350°F/gas 4. Spread the squash or pumpkin in a roasting tin, cover tightly with foil and roast in the hot oven for about 30 minutes until soft. Cool slightly, then scrape the flesh away from the skin and mash to a purée. Season well with salt and leave to cool.

2 In a large bowl, sift together the dry ingredients. In another bowl, combine the milk, egg yolks and melted butter, then beat in the cool squash or pumpkin purée. Put this mixture into the dry ingredients and stir until just combined. Whisk the egg whites until stiff, and fold gently into the squash or pumpkin mixture.

3 Preheat the oven to low. Heat a heavy-based frying pan over a medium heat and add a small dribble of oil. When the oil is hot, gently add a ladleful of batter to form a large pancake, about 12cm (4½in) in diameter. Cook for 2–3 minutes until bubbles appear on the surface, then turn and cook on the other side for 1–2 minutes or until the pancake is spongy and cooked through. Keep warm in the oven while you cook the rest in the same way.

4 To make the topping, mix the pesto with the olive oil to make a dressing. Preheat the grill to medium-high. Place the pancakes on a baking sheet, top each with some goat's cheese and red pepper. Grill for 2–3 minutes until the cheese is bubbling.

5 Transfer the pancakes to individual plates. Top each pancake with a handful of rocket, spoon some pesto dressing over the top and drizzle the balsamic vinegar around the plate. Serve warm.

MAKES ABOUT 6 LARGE PANCAKES; SERVES 3 AS A LIGHT MEAL OR BRUNCH, 6 AS A STARTER

300g (10½oz) butternut squash or pumpkin, seeds removed, cut into 5cm (2in) wedges
125g (4½oz) plain flour
1 tbsp granulated sugar
2 tsp baking powder
½ tsp ground cinnamon
185ml (6½fl oz) milk
2 eggs, separated
40g (1½oz) butter, melted
rapeseed oil or vegetable oil, for frying
salt

FOR THE TOPPING

3 tbsp pesto
3 tbsp extra-virgin olive oil
220g (7½oz) rinded goat's cheese log, thinly sliced
3 red peppers, roasted, skins discarded, torn into strips
90g (3½oz) wild rocket or bitter herbs
2 tbsp good-quality aged balsamic vinegar, or balsamic reduction or syrup

A simple yet delicious recipe for mushrooms on toast with a little hint – no, sorry, a decent hit – of curry powder. It is rich, lush and at the same time has a bite to it. The sauce keeps well, so you can easily prepare it a day in advance. Try also using other mushrooms – the flavours here are good with bolder, stronger mushrooms such as chanterelles.

Cyrus's

MUSHROOM MADRAS BLAZER

MAKES 4–6 SLICES (ENOUGH FOR 2–3 PEOPLE AS A GENEROUS SNACK)

25g (1oz) butter, plus 15g (½oz) for frying the mushrooms, plus extra for buttering the toast
1 small onion, very finely chopped
½–1 mild fresh green chilli, seeds removed, finely chopped
1 garlic clove, finely chopped
1½ tsp Madras curry powder
25g (1oz) plain flour
250ml (9fl oz) vegetable stock, hot
175g (6oz) chestnut mushrooms and/or wild mushrooms, sliced ½cm (¼in) thick
2 tbsp double cream
75g (3oz) Cheddar, grated
1 tbsp chopped fresh coriander
4–6 slices good-quality bread
salt and freshly ground black pepper

1 Melt 25g (1oz) of the butter in a saucepan over a medium heat and when bubbling add the chopped onion, green chilli and garlic. Cook for 5 minutes until softened and golden, then stir in the curry powder and cook for a minute.

2 Remove from the heat, add the flour and mix well – it will become very thick, almost like breadcrumbs. Gradually whisk in the hot vegetable stock to make a very thick sauce. Return the pan to the heat and bring to the boil, stirring, then reduce the heat and simmer for 4–5 minutes to cook out the raw flour, stirring occasionally. By now the sauce will be very thick indeed.

3 Meanwhile, in a frying pan melt 15g (½oz) of the butter over a medium heat, add the sliced mushrooms and cook for 4–5 minutes until just golden. Stir the mushrooms into the sauce along with the cream. Bring the sauce to a simmer, then remove from the heat and stir in the cheese until melted. Season to taste then stir in chopped coriander.

4 Toast the bread and spread one side with butter. Spoon the creamy mushrooms onto the toasted and buttered bread and serve.

What a blast we had when we visited a goat farm down in Wales! Linda and her son, the farmers, showed such care and respect to the animals, and the cheese they produced was fantastic – delicate, not chalky, very fresh and rich. Goat's cheese takes sweetness well, so here we've paired it with an onion marmalade cut with balsamic vinegar and some caraway seeds. These flavours work well with any goat's cheese.

Tony's

GOAT'S CHEESE, RED ONION & CARAWAY SEED TART

1 To make the shortcrust pastry, put the flour and a pinch of salt into a food-processor. Add the butter and lard, and blitz to the consistency of fine breadcrumbs. Transfer this to a mixing bowl. (If you don't have a food-processor, mix the butter and lard into the flour with your fingertips in a mixing bowl.) Stir in 3–4 tablespoons of cold water – just enough to be able to bring the mixture together into a ball.

2 Turn out onto a lightly floured work surface and knead briefly until smooth. Roll out the pastry to a size that will line the base and sides of a 25cm (10in) loose-bottomed flan tin. Press the pastry well into the crease between the base and the sides, prick the pastry base all over with a fork, and chill for 30 minutes. Preheat the oven to 190°C/375°F/gas 5.

3 Line the tart case with baking parchment and fill with baking beans, and blind bake for 15 minutes. Take out, remove the beans and parchment and return the pastry to the oven for a further 10 minutes, or until the base is golden brown. Remove from the oven and set aside.

4 To make the onion marmalade, heat a large frying pan, add the oil and butter and heat until starting to foam. Add the onions, season with salt and pepper, and cook for 5 minutes on a low to medium heat, stirring regularly. Stir in the sugar and cover the pan, then cook for a further 10–15 minutes until the juices have come out of the onions.

5 Uncover the pan and increase the heat, and continue cooking for about 20 minutes to reduce all the juices. While the juices are being reduced, preheat the oven 200°C/400°F/gas 6.

6 When the onion mixture starts to reach the consistency of jam, add the toasted caraway seeds. When the mixture reaches the consistency of marmalade, take the pan off the heat and stir in the vinegar. Adjust the seasoning to taste.

SERVES 4–6

FOR THE SHORTCRUST PASTRY
225g (8oz) plain flour,
    plus extra for kneading
75g (3oz) chilled butter,
    cut into cubes
75g (3oz) chilled lard,
    cut into cubes
salt

FOR THE ONION MARMALADE
1½ tbsp rapeseed oil or
    vegetable oil
80g (3oz) unsalted butter
800g (1lb 14oz) red onions,
    finely sliced
160g (5½oz) caster sugar
1 tbsp caraway seeds,
    toasted in a dry frying pan
80ml (2¾fl oz) balsamic vinegar,
    or more to taste
salt and freshly ground black
    pepper

FOR THE FILLING
2 eggs
200ml (7fl oz) double cream
200g (7oz) goat's cheese, sliced
fresh tarragon and coriander,
    use leaves only, to garnish
salt and freshly ground black
    pepper

Continues overleaf

7 To make the filling, beat the eggs with the cream in a jug or bowl. Mix in the onion marmalade and pour into the blind-baked pastry case. Arrange the goat's cheese on top. Bake in the preheated oven for 30–35 minutes, until set and lightly browned on top.

8 Remove from the oven and leave to cool slightly. Garnish with a scattering of tarragon and coriander leaves, and serve with Spiced Pickled Onions (see page 198).

Tony's
SPICE FOCUS CUMIN

The Ancient Greeks used to grind cumin over food, much as the Brits do black pepper. And there's an idea: why not have a pepper grinder with fresh or toasted cumin seeds in it, perhaps with some coriander as well? Or use my special spice mix in your grinder: toasted cumin seeds, sea salt, a spot of dried thyme perhaps and some chilli powder, if you dare. Try this 'fairy dust' on your chips, or on popcorn or cheese on toast.

Originally coming from Egypt, cumin is now grown in southern Europe, North Africa, Asia, China and parts of the Americas. It belongs to the same family as parsley, caraway and coriander. Like coriander, it flowers in umbrella shapes. When the flowers die, the little seed pods appear, each of which contains one seed. Unlike the round seeds of coriander, cumin seeds are oval and ridged. There are two types of cumin spice, which are very clearly distinguished in Indian cookery: the 'true' or black cumin (quite rare except in specialist shops), and white cumin, which is the seed we commonly buy. Both taste strong, heavy, warm and spicy, and very pungent. Black cumin seeds are darker in colour, slightly smaller than white cumin, and the taste is sweeter and more complex.

Cumin was used by the Ancient Egyptians, Greeks and Romans in medicine as well as cookery. Its main quality was digestive – good for flatulence, according to Dioscorides! – and cumin seeds are still used in the seed mixture, *paan*, served in homes and restaurants after meals.

Cumin is a major crop in Turkey, but India remains the principal producer of the spice, said to be the second most important after the peppercorn. Like coriander, it is best bought whole, given a quick dry-toasting, then ground. Cumin bought pre-ground quickly loses its fragrance.

Ground cumin is used in many meat curries, kebabs and pies, most masalas, and with a lot of Indian and Middle-Eastern vegetable dishes. Sprinkle some ground cumin on lamb before roasting, a great combination, and try lightly ground seeds in gravlax or British poultry dishes. Cumin is a must in the Tex-Mex chilli con carne, and American 'chilli seasonings' are usually a mixture of chilli powder and cumin. I like ground cumin sprinkled on a fried duck's egg (see page 171 for a simple recipe): you could also hard-boil quail's eggs, peel them and then dip them into a mixture of cumin and fine salt. Delicious. Whole, I would use cumin seeds as a condiment for potatoes and aubergines, in the hot oil poured over a lentil dhal, and in yoghurt sauces and garnishes – it's very good in a cucumber raita, for instance. It's also one of the seeds used atop a peshwari naan.

This sounds a bit weird, but forget about the ingredients themselves for a second and just think about their taste – the sweetness of the mango and the salty smokiness of the fish. I am a smoked haddock fiend, I love it, and when you add the sweet mango salsa and crisp pastry it all works together perfectly. Fabulous.

Tony's
SMOKED HADDOCK & MANGO TART

1 Mix all of the mango salsa ingredients together in a bowl. Cover and place in the fridge to marinate for 2 hours (if you have time, leave it for up to 2 days to allow the flavours to develop). Taste and add more chilli, lime juice and a little sugar if you think it's necessary.

2 To make the shortcrust pastry, sift the flour and some salt into a food-processor. Add the chilled butter and lard and work together until the mixture resembles fine breadcrumbs, then transfer to a mixing bowl. If you don't have a food-processor, mix the butter and lard into the flour with your fingertips in a mixing bowl.

3 Stir in a few tablespoons of cold water until the mixture comes together into a ball (you will need about 3–4 tablespoons of water). Turn out onto a lightly floured work surface and knead briefly until smooth. Wrap the dough in clingfilm and put in the fridge to chill for 30 minutes. If you are in a rush, you can use it straight away.

4 With a little butter, grease a 23cm (9in) loose-bottomed flan tin. Roll out the pastry thinly onto a lightly floured work surface, and use to line the prepared tin, leaving any excess pastry hanging over the edges. Prick the base all over with a fork and return it to the fridge to chill for 30 minutes.

5 To make the filling, place the haddock in a pan, cover with water and bring to a simmer. Poach until the haddock is lightly cooked. Remove the fish from the water and set aside to cool. Once cool enough to handle, flake the fish and discard the skin.

6 Preheat the oven to 180°C/350°F/gas 4. Melt the butter for the filling in a large pan, add the leeks and some salt and pepper, and cook gently, uncovered, until tender. Set aside.

SERVES 4–6

FOR THE MANGO SALSA
2 mangoes, cut into 1cm (½in) cubes
2 banana shallots, finely diced
½ red pepper, finely diced
1 fresh green chilli, de-seeded if liked and finely diced
zest and juice of 1 lime
1 bunch tarragon, finely chopped
1 bunch coriander, finely chopped
4cm (1½in) piece fresh green root ginger (mild, young ginger), grated; if not available, use normal root ginger
1 heaped tsp chopped pickled ginger
salt

FOR THE SHORTCRUST PASTRY
225g (8oz) plain flour, plus extra for flouring
75g (3oz) chilled butter, diced, plus extra butter for greasing
75g (3oz) chilled lard, diced
salt

7 Remove the pastry case from the fridge, line the base of the pastry with baking parchment and then fill it with baking beans. Place on a baking sheet and bake blind for 15 minutes. Remove the beans and parchment and return the pastry to the oven for a further 10 minutes, or until the base is golden brown. Reduce the oven to 170°C/335°F/gas 3½ and remove the pastry case.

8 Spoon the leeks over the base of the pastry case, then add about six tablespoons of the mango salsa. Top with the poached smoked haddock. Beat the eggs with the cream in a bowl and add salt and pepper. Pour this mixture over the smoked haddock. Bake for 30–35 minutes, or until just set and lightly browned on top. Remove from the oven and leave to cool slightly before serving with more mango salsa.

FOR THE FILLING
350g (12oz) smoked haddock (peat-smoked if possible, but if not use undyed smoked haddock), skin-on
large knob of butter
2 leeks, thinly sliced
3 eggs
300ml (½ pint) double cream
salt and freshly ground black pepper

I've always loved the simplicity of gravlax, but we've taken it one step further with the addition of peppercorns, coriander seeds, cumin and a little bit of turmeric for colour. What really changes this dish, though, and lifts it from the deep, bass notes of those crushed spices to something really special, are the fresh herbs – mint, dill, tarragon, coriander. Try this with the Peanut and Mint Slaw on page 190, or with some boiled new potatoes, a bit of rapeseed oil and a squeeze of lime.

Tony's
SPĪCED SĪNGH GRAVLAX

1 Mix together all of the marinade ingredients. Spread the marinade over the cut side of the salmon. Tightly wrap the fish in at least three layers of clingfilm.

2 Put the wrapped salmon in a large, shallow tray. Rest a slightly smaller tray or chopping board on top of the fish and weigh it down with something heavy, such as tins of beans. Refrigerate for 48 hours, turning the fish over every 12 hours so.

3 To serve, remove the fish from the briny mixture and slice it thinly, as you would smoked salmon. Arrange a few slices of the gravlax on each plate and serve with some Peanut and Mint Slaw (see page 190).

SERVES 6-10 AS A STARTER
1 side raw salmon
    (about 1.5kg/3lb)

FOR THE MARINADE
large bunch mixed herbs,
    preferably mint, dill,
    coriander and tarragon
60g (2½oz) caster sugar
1 heaped tbsp crushed
    peppercorns, preferably
    white peppercorns
1 heaped tbsp crushed
    coriander seeds
1 tsp crushed roasted fennel
    seeds
1 tsp crushed cumin seeds
¼ tsp turmeric
zest and juice of 1 lemon
    and 1 lime
60g (2½oz) coarse sea salt

This recipe was based around the salmon smokery we visited in Kelso, near Edinburgh (see overleaf) – a master smoker, turning age-old techniques into a science. It tasted sublime, but it was the texture of the fish that we loved the most, and this recipe really brings that out. The crunchiness of the raw beetroot in this salad gives a wonderful contrast to the soft, yielding smoked salmon.

Tony's

SMOKED SALMON WITH SPICED BEETROOT SALAD

1 To make the beetroot salad, whisk together the lime juice and honey in a small bowl. Mix in the smoked paprika and cinnamon, and a pinch of salt. In a separate bowl, mix together the beetroot, raisins and mint leaves and pour the dressing over. Chill in the fridge for an hour. Taste and add more seasoning if necessary.

2 To make the horseradish cream, whisk together the lime juice, honey and horseradish sauce in a small bowl. In a separate bowl, whisk the double cream until soft peaks form when the whisk is removed from the bowl.

3 Stir the horseradish and lime mixture into the whisked cream. Add the chilli powder and salt to taste, and sprinkle on the parsley. Set the salmon slices onto individual plates, and serve with the beetroot salad and a dollop of the horseradish cream.

SERVES 4–6 AS A STARTER
200g (7oz) smoked salmon, sliced

FOR THE BEETROOT SALAD
juice of 1 lime
3 tsp clear honey
½ tsp smoked paprika
¼ tsp ground cinnamon
1 fresh beetroot (about 250g/9oz peeled weight), very finely sliced
3 tbsp raisins, preferably golden
3 heaped tbsp torn mint leaves
salt

FOR THE HORSERADISH CREAM
juice of 2 limes
½ tsp clear honey
4 tbsp horseradish sauce
150ml (¼ pint) double cream
pinch of chilli powder, or more to taste
a small handful of chopped flat-leaf parsley

Tony's
SALMON
SMOKING
KELSO

I've now been fishing twice in my life. The first time was on Loch Awe when I was working at the Ardanaiseig Hotel: city boy, change of weather, not good at rowing, it was a disaster... The second time was on the Tweed just recently, for the television programme. We were by the near-mythic Junction Pool, where the Tweed and the Teviot rivers meet. Apparently, more Atlantic salmon are caught on the fly here than anywhere else in Europe. We caught *nothing*, but I'd happily go again – so long as I don't have to look like a Teletubby in those waders next time!

Afterwards, we went to the nearby Ednam House Hotel, a hotel dedicated to fish and fishermen, where tartan-trousered Ralph Brooks – the owner-proprietor and chef de cuisine – and his French wife, Anne, showed us their smokery. The fish smoked here are either wild, brought in by anglers (from the Tweed and further afield), or farmed. The gutted fish are dry-cured with salt, then the sides or fillets are gently cold-smoked on wire racks over oak chips.

Cyrus and I got to taste some of their newly smoked salmon. It was great, with just the right amount of smoke. It wasn't too salty, and it had a nice yield to the tongue. I made a beetroot salad to go with it, with a horseradish dressing, minimally spiked with chilli. Good smoked salmon doesn't need much.

But I would have loved it if we'd also managed to get our hands on some of the salmon before it went to be smoked! Salmon is one of my favourite fish: it's oily, sturdy, tasty, and takes to spicing very well. My first choice salmon dish would be a gravlax. In Scandinavia they use the cool northern herb, dill, with salt and sugar, and perhaps a dash of akvavit. It's the salt and sugar that do the curing, the dill that flavours. So why not introduce different, spicier flavours? My Singh version on page 39, with a variety of fresh herbs, along with crushed coriander, cumin and fennel seeds, some turmeric and white peppercorns, works really well. Another favourite is spiced salmon fillet: mine is based on an old recipe that my mum used to make, where the salmon is cooked with its marinade (see page 76), and Cyrus has a version that is baked with a herby crust (see page 71). Tuna is the star of a traditional Provençal salade niçoise; I've used salmon (poached with lemon grass) instead, and added spiced instead of plain potatoes (see page 72). And the mayonnaise that accompanies it shows how easy it can be to spice things up: nothing complicated, I've simply added some sweet chilli sauce!

I love smoked salmon, but I'm a smoked haddock man at heart, so I've included two recipes designed for the best, undyed (perhaps even peat-smoked, if you can find it) smoked haddock. Don't ever buy that neon yellow haddock – that's colouring, not smoke. Cyrus smokes fish in his restaurant, over sawdust with added spices such as anise, cassia and bay leaves. It would be fairly easy to try this at home, in a wok, say, with a rack inside and a lid.

When I did my first live cookery demonstration I was feeling nervous with a wee bit of stage fright, so I wanted to make something really simple that I knew wouldn't go wrong – and this is one of my all-time favourites. The sweetness of the shallot marmalade with the ginger and the chilli is finger-licking good. Leave the shells on when you cook the prawns – to eat, peel them off with your fingers and munch on in.

Tony's
HOT & STICKY PRAWNS

1 In a large heavy-bottomed frying pan, heat the oil over medium-high heat. Add the sugar and stir to dissolve, then let the mixture bubble until it starts to caramelise and turn a darker brown – but be careful that it doesn't burn. Add the prawns, shallots and garlic and cook for 2–3 minutes, stirring continuously so they do not burn, until the prawns turn pink.

2 Add the chilli sauce, fish sauce, rice vinegar and tarragon, and cook for 1 minute or until bubbling and the prawns are cooked through. Take the pan off the heat.

3 Put all of the salad ingredients except the oil and seasoning into a large bowl. Dribble over the olive oil and season to taste, then toss to mix. Serve the salad with the prawns, and spoon round any excess sauce from the pan. Serve at once.

SERVES 4

2 tbsp rapeseed oil or vegetable oil
50g (2oz) palm sugar, finely chopped, or 40g (1½oz) soft light brown sugar
300g (10½oz) raw peeled prawns
100g (4oz) shallots, finely chopped
1 garlic clove, finely chopped
50ml (2fl oz) sweet Thai chilli sauce
1 tsp Thai fish sauce, or more to taste
40ml (1¾fl oz) rice vinegar
2 tbsp chopped fresh tarragon

FOR THE SALAD
100g (4oz) rocket
small yellow pepper, seeds removed, finely chopped
40g (1½oz) pickled sushi ginger, well drained and finely chopped
2 tbsp olive oil
salt and freshly ground black pepper

FĪSH

& A BĪT OF SEAFOOD

Pancakes: such simple things that, if done well, can be magical. Call them what you will – crêpes, griddle cakes, hot cakes, flapjacks, whatever – as soon as you pour that batter onto a hot pan, it comes alive with taste. Add the smokiness of the haddock and the tart, zingy salsa and you have a moreish light meal that you can come back to again and again. Try swapping the haddock for any other filling that you can think of – anything goes, it's that good.

Tony's

HADDOCK PANCAKE WITH ZINGY SALSA

1 To make the pancake batter, sift the flour and a pinch of salt into a bowl, and make a well in the centre. Gradually whisk in the egg and milk, incorporating the flour from the sides, and combine to a smooth batter. Set the mixture aside to rest while you continue with the recipe.

2 Mix together all of the soured cream ingredients except the lime juice. When mixed, add lime juice to taste, along with some salt and pepper. Set aside in the fridge.

3 Put all of the salsa ingredients except for the lime juice and olive oil in a food-processor. Pulse to create a rough purée, then tip the mixture into a bowl and season to taste with lime juice and a little salt and pepper. Mix in olive oil to taste, then add more salt, pepper or lime juice as required. Set aside.

4 You can now make the pancakes. Preheat the oven to minimum. Heat an 18cm (7in) pancake pan and add a dot of butter, using kitchen paper to smear it around the pan. Measure out about 2 tablespoons of the pancake mixture into a ladle, then pour this into the pan and quickly swirl it around the base – there should be just enough to thinly cover the bottom of the pan. Cook for a few seconds until brown, flip onto the other side for a few seconds until brown, then slide onto a warm plate and keep warm in the oven.

5 Wipe the pan clean and continue cooking pancakes in the same way until you have a total of 8 pancakes.

SERVES 4 (2 PER PERSON)

FOR THE PANCAKES
100g (4oz) plain flour
1 egg, lightly beaten
285ml (½ pint) milk,
　at room temperature
salt and freshly ground black
　pepper
lightly salted butter, melted,
　for frying

FOR THE SOURED CREAM
125ml (4½fl oz) soured cream
1 tbsp sweet chilli sauce
25g (1oz) chopped fresh chives
1 heaped tbsp chopped fresh
　tarragon
¼ red onion, finely diced
1 tbsp lime juice
　(juice of about ½ lime)

Continues overleaf

6 To make the filling, heat the oil in a large heavy-bottomed non-stick pan, then add the haddock pieces. Cook the pieces, without stirring, until the bottoms have a nice golden brown colour; then turn the pieces over, add the butter and cook until that side is golden. When the fish is nearly done, add 2 teaspoons of salsa verde per person and cook for a further minute. Don't be alarmed if the fish breaks up a little.

7 Divide the fish between the pancakes and roll each pancake like a spring roll. Serve on a plate with the baby spinach and soured cream.

FOR THE SALSA VERDE

30g (1¼oz) fresh coriander, including stalks
30g (1¼oz) each sprigs of fresh flat-leaf parsley, tarragon, basil and mint; strip off the leaves and discard the stems
1 garlic clove
2 anchovies
15g (½oz) capers
15g (½oz) small gherkins
lime juice, to taste
40ml (1¾fl oz) extra-virgin olive oil, or to taste

FOR THE PANCAKE FILLING

1½ tbsp vegetable or sunflower oil
500g (1lb 2oz) undyed smoked haddock, skinned and de-boned, cut into 8 equal pieces
20g (¾oz) lightly salted butter
100g (4oz) baby spinach, to serve

In all honesty, I do not know the full origins of this tamarind-flavoured dish. We Parsees make something similar, but it's also common in Goa, Kerala and other regions. I really enjoy the use of tamarind here, as I would normally expect to see tamarind used with fish in Chinese, Thai or Vietnamese dishes. To use it in an Indian meal like this just shows how spices can move across cultures.

Cyrus's
FISH WITH A ZING & ZANG

1 Rinse the fish and pat dry with kitchen paper, and place in a dish. Squeeze the lime over the fillets and sprinkle with half of the turmeric, then mix well and set aside. With a pestle and mortar, crush the coriander seeds to a powder and set aside. Grind the cashew nuts in the pestle and mortar with a splash of water to make a creamy paste, transfer to a bowl then set aside.

2 In a food-processor or mini-chopper, blitz together the ground coriander seeds, cumin, garlic and the remaining turmeric, adding a splash of water if necessary. Add this to the cashew paste and mix well to form a smooth spice paste (masala).

3 Heat the oil in a casserole dish, add the onion and a pinch of salt, and cook gently until coloured and softened. Add the chillies and stir, and after a few seconds add the masala and sauté well to cook the masala and ensure the spices get well absorbed. The masala is ready when it is well browned and oil begins to show at the edges. Watch it as it is cooking as it may well stick to the bottom of the pan; remedy this by adding a tablespoon or so of water every so often.

4 Meanwhile, mix the tamarind paste with the jaggery or sugar and 250ml (9fl oz) of water, and stir well. When the masala is ready, add the tamarind mix and bring to the boil, then simmer until the sauce reaches the consistency of single cream; the masala is fully cooked when the chilli in the sauce does not hit the throat when tasted. Adjust the seasoning to taste.

5 Gently add the fish pieces and simmer for 3–5 minutes. Then cover the pan, turn off the heat and let the fish rest for a few minutes to cook thoroughly. Serve with rice and a prepared green chilli to garnish.

SERVES 2

250g (9oz) white fish fillets, such as sea bass or bream, cut into 7.5cm (3in) pieces
juice of ½ lime
1 tsp turmeric
1 tbsp coriander seeds
2 tbsp natural cashew nuts
1 tsp cumin seeds
3–4 garlic cloves
2 tbsp sunflower oil
1 onion, thinly sliced
1–3 fresh green chillies, seeds removed if liked, thinly sliced, plus 1 fresh green chilli per person for garnish, seeds removed, and sliced lengthways with stalk intact
2–3 tbsp tamarind paste
1 tbsp jaggery (Indan raw cane sugar), or 1 heaped tsp soft brown sugar
pinch of salt

Marinades are a great way to get the flavours of spice into food. Indian cuisine uses many different marinades, but not usually with cheese! It may sound like a strange addition, but believe me it is delicious.

Cyrus's
CREAMY CHEDDARY GRILLED FISH

1 To make the marinade, crush the garlic and ginger together with a pestle and mortar. You should have 1 tbsp of mixture. Place this and all of the remaining marinade ingredients except the ground almonds in a food-processor or blender, and blitz to a fine paste. If the mixture seems a little runny add the ground almonds; this will help the marinade to stick to the fish.

2 Pat the fish dry with kitchen paper, season with salt and pepper and spread the marinade over both sides. Place the fish on a tray, cover with clingfilm and refrigerate for a couple of hours.

3 Preheat the grill to high and brush some oil over the grill rack to prevent the fish from sticking. Put a tray beneath the rack to catch any marinade during cooking. Grill the fish for 5–6 minutes each side; when cooked the fish should be nicely browned and the flesh opaque. Gather up the juices and marinade from the tray and add to the dish with a spritz of lemon juice. Serve with buttered rice.

SERVES 2

2 x 400–500g (14oz–1lb 2oz) whole sea bass, bream or sole, cleaned, gutted, scaled, fins removed and gashed diagonally on both sides; if using sole, remove the dark skin
rapeseed oil or vegetable oil, to brush
fresh lemon, to serve
salt and freshly ground black pepper

FOR THE MARINADE

2 garlic cloves
2cm (¾in) piece fresh root ginger
100ml (3½fl oz) double cream
100g (4 oz) Greek-style natural yoghurt
100g (4oz) strong Cheddar, grated
¼ tsp ground nutmeg or freshly grated nutmeg
¼ tsp ground mace
6 cardamom pods, crushed to a powder with a pestle and mortar (¼ tsp)
1 green bird's-eye chilli
50g (2oz) ground almonds (optional)
½ tsp salt, or to taste

Cyrus's
SPICE FOCUS NUTMEG

The name 'nutmeg' comes originally from the Latin words for 'nut' and 'musk', and the perfume of nutmeg is indeed musky, warm and sweet, so is well-suited to both sweet and savoury dishes. It is vital in a béchamel, but goes just as well in a custard. You can use it in potato dishes, with spinach, in soups, curries, egg dishes and a multitude of drinks and chutneys. I often use it in fish dishes, and it features in our recipe for Coronation chicken (see page 97). Along with rosewater, it flavours the baked egg custard that is traditionally served at Parsee weddings: when set, it's cut into pieces, and served at the beginning of the meal. (We like to start and finish joyous occasions on sweet notes!)

Nutmeg is quite expensive, so my mum didn't use it much, except in her caramel custard and some fudges. She kept it in a tiny 1930s jar, which I still have at home.

The nutmeg tree is unique in producing a brace of spices: nutmeg and mace. *Myristica fragrans* is a medium to large evergreen tree, which used to grow only in the Moluccas archipelago in Indonesia. The 'mystical fragrance' of the trees and their fruits was so potent that you could apparently smell the islands from ten miles out to sea! Nowadays the trees are grown elsewhere in the tropics, notably Grenada in the West Indies.

The fruit of the nutmeg tree is the size of an apricot. When ripe, the outer flesh splits open, revealing the seed. This brown shiny seed is encased in a lacy red membrane, the aril, which when dried gives us mace. The nutmeg seed itself is dried for a month or so, until the inner kernel rattles inside its shell. The shell is removed and the kernel is ready for use. When fresh, you can actually see the essential oil of the nutmeg – I squeezed some onto my fingers on camera – but even after drying, you can test for freshness. Press a needle into the nutmeg: if you can see a little oil, it's good. Always buy whole nutmegs and grate them yourself.

Mace, sold in yellow blades (the dried arils) or ground, adds a milder but still pungent nutmeg flavour to pies, pâtés, sausages and stuffings. Tony knows, of course, that both nutmeg and mace are essential flavourings in that Scottish favourite, haggis. Toast mace first in a low oven, to slowly draw the moisture out, then grind in an electric grinder.

When nutmeg was most valued in Europe, the wealthy used to grate nutmeg over drinks and foods because of its supposed protective medical properties. The diarist Samuel Pepys used a few gratings in a spoonful of honey to allay cold symptoms, and it's said that nutmeg can, if taken in excess, bring on hallucinogenic episodes.

This dish is a little bit fiddly, but the good news is that you can get all of the tricky work done a day in advance. Make the spicy butter and keep it cool, and get your fish parcels ready and in the fridge. When you're ready to serve it, all the hard work's been done – just take it out, roast it and you're good to go. A great party piece.

Tony's

ROAST FISH WITH SPICY BUTTER

1 First make the coriander butter. Put the butter in a bowl, add all of the remaining ingredients and beat until it all comes together. Scrape the mixture onto a piece of clingfilm or greaseproof paper, roll it into a sausage shape and put it into the fridge to chill (or the freezer for a short while, if you're in a hurry).

2 Preheat the oven to 200°C/400°F/gas 6. On a piece of aluminium foil large enough to cover the base of a roasting tin, lay out the bacon so that it covers the foil and the rashers overlap slightly. Sprinkle with pepper and place the sage leaves on top of the bacon. Now place the hake in the centre; if using two fillets place one on top of the other, with some sage leaves tucked between the two. Fold the bacon over the fish so that it envelops it in a parcel. Tuck any loose ends underneath the fish.

3 Lift the piece of foil, with everything still on top of it, and place it in a roasting tin. Drizzle with the oil and roast on the top shelf of the oven for 20 minutes, or until some of the milky white liquid has escaped from the fish and the flesh is opaque. If you want the bacon extra crisp then flash it under a hot grill for 1–2 minutes at the end of cooking.

4 To prepare the watercress, heat the oil in a frying pan over a medium heat, toss in the watercress and fry the watercress for 1–2 minutes until just wilted. Squeeze over the lemon juice. Serve the fish with the watercress and top with a couple of slices of the spiced butter; you can pop the plate under the grill or into the oven for about 30 seconds if you want the butter to melt a little. Serve with some boiled new potatoes.

SERVES 6

200g (7oz) smoked streaky bacon
20g (¾oz) sage leaves
1 x 1kg (2lb 4oz) hake fillet, skinned and deboned; if not available, use 2 x 500g (1lb 2oz) fillets
1 tbsp rapeseed oil or vegetable oil
freshly ground black pepper

FOR THE CORIANDER BUTTER

125g (4½oz) unsalted butter, softened to room temperature
1 small garlic clove, finely crushed
1 tbsp honey
1½ tbsp coarse grain mustard
a few drops Tabasco
1 tbsp whisky
25g (1oz) fresh coriander, chopped
1½ tbsp coriander seeds, toasted in a dry frying pan and lightly crushed
salt

FOR THE WATERCRESS

1 tbsp rapeseed oil or vegetable oil
300g (10½oz) watercress
juice of 1 lemon

For Indian people, food needs to have a little zing here and little zing there, and now we have influenced the British palate, too. This recipe for zingy fish and chips is simple to make and so satisfying for the soul. We made this dish when we visited Hastings, where local fish include bream, whiting and Dover sole, but select the fish you prefer; for this recipe fillets work best. Always try to use only sustainable British fish, approved by the Marine Conservation Society.

Cyrus

TODĪWALA & SĪNGH'S SPĪCED FĪSH & CHĪPS

1 In a large bowl, mix together all of the marinade ingredients until the salt has completely dissolved. Taste and adjust the seasoning to your liking. Spread each fillet thoroughly with marinade, place the fillets on a flat dish in which all the fish can fit, cover and chill for a few hours or overnight.

2 A chilled batter will have a better texture, so put the flour in the bowl in which you will mix up the batter, stir in the crushed peppercorns and a little salt, and refrigerate until you are ready to cook – or better still, place in the freezer if space allows. Also chill the lemonade before cooking, and mix together the ingredients for the spicy chip seasoning and set aside.

3 To make the chips, peel the potatoes and cut them into 1cm (½in) thick 'fingers'. Put these in a pan of cold water with plenty of salt, and bring to the boil. Cook until soft when pressed with a knife. Drain and cool in the colander. Pat dry.

4 Heat the oil or dripping in a deep-fat fryer or heavy-based saucepan to 150°C/300°F. Do not leave the hot oil unattended. Cook the chips in batches for about 6 minutes each batch, or until the chips are turning lightly yellowish. Carefully remove and drain on a dish lined with kitchen paper. Preheat the oven to minimum.

5 Increase the temperature of the oil in the fryer to 180°C/350°F and fry the chips again to a beautiful brown colour. Drain well on kitchen paper, then dust with the spicy seasoning. Keep the chips warm in the oven, and place another baking tray inside to warm up.

SERVES 6

6 single-portion fillets of your
    preferred white fish, wiped dry

FOR THE MARINADE
juice of 1 lime or lemon
1 tsp turmeric
2 tsp ground cumin
1 tbsp ground coriander
1 heaped tsp red chilli powder
4 garlic cloves, well crushed
1 tbsp Worcestershire sauce
2 heaped tsp salt,
    preferably sea salt

FOR THE BATTER
400g (14oz) self-raising flour
1 tsp peppercorns, crushed
500–600ml (17fl oz–1 pint)
    traditional cloudy lemonade
pinch of salt

FOR THE SPICY CHIP SEASONING
1 tsp red chilli powder
½ tsp ground cumin
1 tsp salt

Continues overleaf

6 When all of the chips are ready, you can make the batter and cook the fish. Keep the oil in the fryer at 180°C/350°F. To make the batter, whisk the cold lemonade into the chilled seasoned flour.

7 Dip a portion of fish into the batter and carefully lower it into the hot oil. Fry for 4–6 minutes, or until crisp and golden brown. Transfer to the empty tray in the oven. Continue to cook all of the fish in the same way. Serve the fish with the spicy chips.

NOTES: A drizzling of lime or lemon juice on the chips makes them even tastier – no vinegar for us. Another excellent addition would be a smooth and spicy mayonnaise dressing.

You don't have to batter and deep-fry the marinated fish; it would also be delicious pan-fried, meunièred (served with browned butter, lemon juice and parsley), or just plain grilled.

FOR THE CHIPS
1.5kg (3lb) potatoes, or more to taste (I am a Parsee, we thrive on potatoes), preferably Maris Piper or Rudolph Red but not new potatoes
rapeseed oil, vegetable oil or dripping, for deep-fat frying
salt

This flavoursome and robust curry was demonstrated to me by Mrs Kutti, our host on my last visit to Kerala; it is easily adaptable to all seafood and also chicken. Coconut oil is commonly used in the coastal regions of India, but you can use rapeseed oil or vegetable oil if you prefer.

Cyrus's
CREAMY FISH CURRY

1 Heat the oil in a wok or large pan over a medium-high heat until the oil hazes. Add the ginger, garlic and green chillies. Cook for 30 seconds or so, reduce the heat to medium and add the sliced onions and a generous teaspoon of salt, and cook for a few minutes to soften the onion.

2 Add the curry leaves and the turmeric, if using, and cook for 1–2 minutes, then add the fish steaks and cook well on both sides, being careful not to break up the fish. Move the fish to the side of the pan, add the crushed cardamom, cloves and peppercorns, and cook for a further 1–2 minutes.

3 Add the tomatoes and the diluted coconut milk, bring to the boil and simmer for a couple of minutes. Add the second tin of coconut milk and bring the curry back to the boil, and adjust the seasoning to taste. Boil until the sauce has thickened a little, then stir through the vinegar, coriander and lime juice, if using, and leave it to stand for a few minutes before serving. If the sauce is too thin, remove the fish to a warm dish and boil the sauce gently in the pan to reduce the liquor, then pour it over the fish. Serve with steamed rice.

SERVES 6

3 tbsp coconut oil, rapeseed oil or vegetable oil
1 heaped tbsp grated ginger
1 tbsp crushed garlic (about 3 cloves)
2 green finger chillies, deseeded if liked, cut into four
2 small onions, sliced
4–5 fresh curry leaves, either whole or shredded
1 tsp turmeric (optional)
1kg (2lb 4oz) firm-fleshed fish steaks, such as bream or sea bass
3–4 cardamom pods, crushed with a pestle and mortar
3–4 cloves, crushed with a pestle and mortar
1 tbsp crushed black peppercorns
2 tomatoes, skinned and seeds removed, diced
2 x 400ml (14fl oz) tins coconut milk, one tin diluted with one tin of water
1 tbsp palm vinegar or cider vinegar (optional)
1–2 tbsp chopped fresh coriander (optional)
juice of ½ a lime (optional)
salt

This is very hearty, a real rib-sticker of a dish – the sort of thing that a Wild West cowboy would definitely eat. It's very simple, a lot of fun to make, and the fish goes so well with the spicy baked beans. Dab can be found in larger supermarkets and is well worth searching out, but if you can't get hold of any of the options below try some sea bream fillets instead.

Tony's

FISH WITH WILD WEST BEANS

1 First prepare the beans. Heat the oil in a heavy-based pan and gently cook the onions until they start to colour. Add the chopped garlic and ginger, and continue cooking until everything starts to colour. Add the chilli, garam masala and 150ml (¼ pint) of water, and continue cooking until nearly all the water is gone.

2 Add the baked beans, bring to a slow simmer and cook for 5 minutes. Add a squeeze of lemon juice and salt to taste. Keep warm while you cook the fish.

3 Mix together the Parmesan, parsley and coriander, and set aside. Pat the fish dry with kitchen paper and season well with salt and pepper. Heat the oil in a frying pan and, working in batches if necessary to avoid overcrowding the pan, cook the fish on one side for 2–3 minutes. Turn the fish over and add the butter. When it foams and turns golden, baste the fish and cook for a further 3–5 minutes.

4 Add the capers to the pan and cook for a further 2 minutes, continually spooning the butter over the fish. Remove the fish from the pan, and add the parsley mixture and a squeeze of lemon. Serve with the baked beans.

SERVES 4
75g (3oz) Parmesan
2 tbsp chopped fresh
   flat-leaf parsley
2 tbsp chopped coriander
4–6 fillets meaty white fish
   such as dab, coley, dogfish
   or sea bream
3 tbsp olive oil
100g (4oz) butter
3 tbsp capers
½ lemon
salt and freshly ground
   black pepper

FOR THE WILD WEST BEANS
1 tbsp rapeseed oil or
   vegetable oil
3 small red onions, finely
   chopped
4 garlic cloves, finely chopped
2.5cm (1in) piece fresh root
   ginger, finely chopped
1 tsp finely chopped fresh
   green chilli
1 tsp garam masala
1 x 420g (14oz) tin baked beans
squeeze of lemon juice

This recipe is a very versatile one, and would work just as well with a variety of fish. Any sweet, meaty white fish, such as hake, cod and John Dory would make a good alternative, or you could try sea bass or bream fillets if you want a lighter option. If you're using bass or bream you can skip the oven stage, and simply fry them in the pan: start them off skin-side down, then cook for a few minutes on the flesh side.

Tony's

DOVER SOLE WITH LIME & GINGER

1 Bring a large pan of salted water to the boil, drop in the asparagus and simmer for 3 minutes or until just tender. Remove from the water, drain and set aside.

2 To prepare the fish, heat the oven to 200°C/400°F/gas 6. Mix together the flour, chilli powder and some salt and pepper, and dust the fish in it, then shake off any excess. Heat a large, non-stick, ovenproof frying pan over a medium-high heat; use two frying pans if the fish are too large to fit in a single pan. (If you have no ovenproof pans, then preheat a lightly oiled baking sheet.) Add the oil and heat it until it hazes. Add the sole (skin-side down if you've part-skinned them) and fry, without moving them, for 3–4 minutes until they form a golden crust. Turn over and transfer the frying pan to the top of the hot oven (or transfer the fish to the warmed baking sheet and place in the oven), and cook for a further 8–10 minutes until cooked through and the flesh is opaque.

3 For the sauce, melt the butter in a frying pan over a medium heat, and let it bubble for 2–3 minutes until it turns a nut-brown colour. Reduce the heat to low, add the ginger, lime juice, pomegranate seeds and chopped coriander and warm it through; don't overheat it or it will separate. Season to taste. Serve the sole with the asparagus and spoon the sauce over the top.

SERVES 2

12 asparagus spears
4 tbsp plain flour
1 tsp chilli powder
2 Dover sole, scaled, cleaned and trimmed (dark skin removed if you can, otherwise you could slash it in several places with a sharp knife), or other fish of your choice
1–2 tbsp vegetable or rapeseed oil
salt and freshly ground black pepper

FOR THE SAUCE

140g (5oz) unsalted butter
50g (2oz) chopped fresh root ginger
4 tbsp lime juice (about 3 limes)
30g (1¼oz) fresh pomegranate seeds
2 tbsp chopped fresh coriander

A delicate blend of spices, but one that works magically with salmon – especially wild salmon, if you can get it. For a smoother crust, grind the spices in a pestle and mortar before adding them to the food processor.

Cyrus's

INDIAN HERB-CRUSTED SALMON

1 First make the crust topping. Blitz the bread in a food-processor to a soft crumb consistency. Add all of the remaining crust ingredients, and blitz again until you have a green crumb mixture. Taste the mixture, adjust the seasoning to personal preference and set aside.

2 To make the marinade, mix together the turmeric, salt and lemon juice. Apply it well all over the fish. The fish can be cooked immediately, but if time allows, cover and refrigerate for 2–3 hours to allow the flavours in the marinade to mature.

3 Preheat the oven to 180°C/350°F/gas 4, and place a rack near the top of the oven. Drain the fish well of any liquid and dab dry with kitchen paper.

4 Heat the tablespoon of rapeseed oil or vegetable oil in a heavy-based frying pan over a medium-high heat, and fry the fish fillets skin-side down, without moving them, for 2–3 minutes until the skin is crisp and browned. (You may need to do this in two or three batches to avoid overcrowding the pan, which results in soggy skin.) Turn the fillets over and cook on the flesh side for a minute or so.

5 Transfer the fish, skin-side up, to a roasting tray. Place them close to one another, and spoon the crumb mixture over to coat all the pieces in a nice thick layer. Drizzle over the olive or rapeseed oil, place the tray in the oven and in about 6–8 minutes your crust should be ready and your salmon cooked to medium. If you like a crisper crust or your salmon fully cooked through, then leave the dish in a few minutes more, but the fish should be in the oven no longer than 10–12 minutes in total. Serve with boiled new potatoes and a salad.

SERVES 6

6 x 150g (5oz) salmon fillets, skin on
1 tbsp rapeseed oil or vegetable oil, for frying
50ml (2fl oz) extra-virgin olive oil or cold-pressed extra-virgin rapeseed oil

FOR THE CRUST
150g (5oz) fresh white bread, crust removed
a large handful of fresh coriander
3 garlic cloves
¾ tsp cumin seeds
1 tsp coriander seeds
1 tsp dried thyme, or 1 sprig of fresh thyme
1 mild green chilli, seeds removed if liked, chopped
½ tsp salt
50ml (2fl oz) rapeseed oil or vegetable oil

FOR THE MARINADE
1 tsp turmeric
½ tsp salt
2 tbsp lemon or lime juice

There are classics and then there are classics, and niçoise hasn't changed much at all in all of the years that I've been cooking. What could make this tried-and-tested-dish even better? Some Scotch salmon and Bombay aloo. The spicy potato just elevates it to another level.

Tony's

SALMON NIÇOISE WITH BOMBAY ALOO

1 To make the Bombay aloo, cook the potatoes in a pan of boiling salted water until cooked but still firm. Use a slotted spoon to remove them from the water and set aside to dry out. Retain the cooking water.

2 Over a medium heat, heat 1 tablespoon of the oil in a frying pan and fry the cumin, mustard and sesame seeds until they start to pop. Transfer the seeds to a small plate, retaining the oil in the pan. Put the ginger in the pan and fry for 1 minute, then set aside with the popped seeds.

3 Heat the remaining tablespoon of oil in the frying pan and gently cook the onion until softening but still opaque, then add the turmeric, chilli powder and mango powder if using (but not the lemon juice), and cook for a further 2 minutes.

4 Add the popped seeds and cooked ginger and stir. Add a splash of the potato cooking water, and some lemon juice if no mango powder was used, then stir in the garam masala. Increase the heat and add the potatoes, and stir gently until fully coated and dry. Season with salt.

5 To prepare the salad, cook the eggs in rapidly boiling water: quail's eggs for exactly 2 minutes, hen's eggs for 3½ minutes. Remove with a slotted spoon and plunge into cold water for a few minutes until cool enough to peel by hand. Set aside.

6 Put all the remaining salad ingredients except the coriander leaves in a bowl. Mix together the vinaigrette ingredients, and dress the salad generously. Mix well and divide between 4 wide serving bowls or plates, then set aside. Make the Thai mayonnaise by mixing together the two ingredients and set aside.

7 To cook the salmon, put the stock, thyme, lime and lemon grass in a large pan and bring to a simmer. Continue to simmer for 5–10 minutes

SERVES 4

FOR THE BOMBAY ALOO
300g (10½oz) potatoes, peeled and cut into bite-size cubes
2 tbsp rapeseed oil or vegetable oil
1 tsp cumin seeds
1 tsp mustard seeds
1 tsp sesame seeds
15g (½oz) chopped fresh root ginger
½ large onion, diced
1 tsp turmeric
½ tsp chilli powder
1 tsp mango powder (if available, otherwise use a squeeze of lemon juice)
1 tsp garam masala
salt

FOR THE SALAD
16 quail's eggs or 4 hen's eggs, at room temperature
200g (7oz) fine French beans, blanched in boiling water and refreshed in cold water
24 cherry tomatoes, cut in half
24 plump black olives, stoned
2 large shallots, sliced into rings
a small handful of fresh coriander leaves

Continues overleaf

so that the flavours infuse. Add the salmon fillets and poach gently for 5–10 minutes; remove the pan from the heat and leave to cool for a few minutes.

8   Remove the fillets from the poaching liquor and flake one onto each salad bowl or plate. Slice the peeled eggs in two and add to the salad. Top each serving with some Bombay aloo, sprinkle coriander leaves over and serve with the Thai mayonnaise.

FOR THE CLASSIC VINAIGRETTE
1 tsp Dijon mustard
1 tbsp white wine vinegar
3½ tbsp olive oil

FOR THE THAI MAYONNAISE
4 tbsp mayonnaise
1 tbsp sweet chilli sauce
   or sriracha sauce

FOR THE SALMON
1.5 litres (2½ pints) fish stock
a few sprigs of fresh thyme
4 slices of lime
4 lemon grass sticks,
   bruised and roughly chopped
4 x 150g (5oz) salmon fillets,
   skinned and boned

This is my absolute favourite. If someone was to ask me what my signature dish was, this is it, stolen – sorry, 'borrowed' – from my mum. When we were growing up we didn't have much money, so she would send us down to the fishmonger to ask for the leftover salmon bones and heads. She'd work her magic and make them absolutely delicious – even now when I make this dish at home, I still use some salmon bones alongside the fillet. This is the best spiced salmon dish you'll ever try.

Tony's

PUNJABĪ SPĪCED SALMON

1 Mix all of the marinade ingredients together. Add the salmon, toss to coat in the marinade, cover and chill for 1 hour or overnight.

2 When ready to prepare the meal, cook the rice in a large pan of boiling water for 8–10 minutes until tender but holding its shape. When cooked, drain then gently fold in the chopped herbs and season with salt to taste. Set aside and keep warm.

3 To cook the fish, heat the rapeseed oil or vegetable oil in a pan over a medium-high heat, add the carom or fenugreek seeds and swirl for 30 seconds, then add the salmon, skin-side down, and spoon its marinade around it. Cook for 3–4 minutes each side, or until just cooked through (or cooked to your liking). To serve, spoon some rice on warm serving plates. Top with the fish and spoon around the sauce from the salmon. Serve with some roasted cherry tomatoes.

SERVES 4

4 x 150g (5oz) salmon fillets, skin on
1 tbsp rapeseed oil or vegetable oil
1 tsp carom seeds or ½ tsp fenugreek seeds

FOR THE MARINADE

200g (7oz) leeks, finely diced
250g (9oz) tinned chopped tomatoes
4 garlic cloves, finely chopped
4 fresh mild green chillies, seeds removed, finely chopped
7cm (2¾in) piece fresh root ginger, finely grated
1 tsp turmeric
1 tsp garam masala
salt

FOR THE RICE

280g (10oz) basmati rice, washed well
30g (1oz) finely chopped fresh tarragon
30g (1oz) finely chopped fresh chives
30g (1oz) finely chopped fresh coriander

Prawns, rice and spices. What more to say? I love this dish and, though I've put it in here as a main course, I'm a greedy so-and-so – I eat this as a side dish! A helping of pilaf, a couple of roasted Toulouse sausages, a dollop of crème fraîche on the side. Wonderful.

Tony's
PRAWN PĪLAF

1 Heat a large pan and melt half of the butter in it, add the onion and carrot, and cook over a medium heat for 6–7 minutes until lightly browned. Add the tomato purée and stock, bring to the boil and simmer for 15 minutes.

2 Strain the stock into a measuring jug; you need 650ml (1 pint 2fl oz) of strained stock. If there is more than this, return it to the pan and boil rapidly until reduced to this amount; if less than 650ml, then top up with more fresh stock. (You can keep the leftover onions and carrots and use them as a side dish with another meal.)

3 Rinse the rice in a few changes of cold water until the water runs relatively clear. Melt the remaining butter in a large, heavy-based saucepan and add the garlic, cloves, cardamom and cinnamon and fry gently for 5 minutes. Stir in the turmeric and cook for a further minute.

4 Add the rice and stir well to coat. Add the strained stock, season with salt and bring to the boil, then turn the heat right down to the slightest simmer, put a lid on the pan and leave to simmer for 10 minutes – do not lift the lid during this time. After 10 minutes the rice should be cooked and fluffy and all the moisture absorbed; if not, place the lid back on and leave on a very low heat for a further 2–3 minutes.

5 Heat the rapeseed oil or vegetable oil in a frying pan over medium-high heat, add the prawns and cook for 3–4 minutes, stirring once or twice, until they have turned pink and are cooked through. Strain off any liquid.

6 Uncover the rice and gently stir in the hot prawns, coriander, diced tomatoes and lemon juice, if using. Season to taste with salt and pepper and serve.

SERVES 4

50g (2oz) butter
1 small onion, chopped
1 small carrot, roughly chopped
1 tsp tomato purée
1 litre (1¾ pints) chicken or vegetable stock
350g (12oz) basmati rice
5 garlic cloves, very finely chopped
3 cloves
3 cardamom pods, bruised with a rolling pin
10cm (4in) piece cinnamon stick, broken into 4 pieces
½ tsp turmeric
1 tbsp rapeseed oil or vegetable oil
400–500g (14oz–1lb 2oz) peeled, raw prawns
3 tbsp chopped fresh coriander
3 plum tomatoes, skinned, de-seeded and diced
juice of 1 lemon (optional)
salt and freshly ground black pepper

SPICE FOCUS CINNAMON

Cinnamon is a warm, earthy and sweet spice, fragrant, with hints of citrus and clove. We bake with it in the West: it's good in drop scones, Christmas buns and cakes. My mum used to put it in her shortbread, which my friends didn't like (an Indian step too far, perhaps), but it shows that she was definitely reintroducing the Brits to spices before I was! It appears in desserts, fruit pies, crumbles (wonderful with rhubarb or apple), and mulled drinks (great in the spiced rum on page 240). I like it with black pepper and mint in a dish of strawberries, and who doesn't appreciate teatime buttered toast sprinkled with ground cinnamon!

In the subcontinent, cinnamon is used in curries, and meat and poultry stews of all kinds: its distinctive flavour can be found in a wide range of dishes. Cinnamon is ground in garam masala. We used it in a masala paste for lamb meatballs (see page 153), but if you kept excess paste in the fridge (covered with a little oil), you could smear it over pork chops or chicken legs for a simple, instant spicy dinner.

True cinnamon – *Cinnamomum verum* – comes from Sri Lanka. Like cassia (see page 128), the spice is the aromatic bark of an evergreen tree belonging to the laurel family.

Cinnamon is harvested from young trees, which are coppiced to keep them small. Shoots grow from the cut bases, and are harvested in the rainy season at six months. The outer bark is removed and discarded, and the inner bark is cut from the trunk – a highly specialised job, requiring a lot of skill. This very thin inner bark is then packed together with other shoot layers and left to dry, at which point they curl up into the familiar quill shape of the spice. (Cinnamon can be differentiated from cassia because of these thin layers; cassia has only one thickish layer.) They're then cut down to size before being sold, but these quills can actually be up to a metre long, something that amazed the team when we filmed the television series! To give the bark time to grow again, the tree is left to regenerate for a couple of years: amazingly, a good tree can produce for up to 200 years.

Cinnamon and cassia have been known and used in cooking and medicine for thousands of years, by the Ancient Egyptians, Greeks and Romans, and are mentioned in old Chinese and Indian medical texts. Cinnamon is frequently used in *masala chais*, or spiced teas, and the principal importer of cinnamon is said to be Mexico, where it is frequently used to flavour drinks of coffee and chocolate. Even stirring your own coffee, tea or hot chocolate with a cinnamon stick could spice up your cuppa quite a bit...

Stuffed king prawns are hugely popular in Goa, and several recipes have evolved there. Here is my own, taken from various experiences meeting some fabulous cooks, and trying my best to learn a few bits and bobs here and there. This is traditionally cooked in banana leaf and served with a coconut curry, but I've found that foil parcels give perfect results.

Cyrus's
STUFFED KING PRAWNS

1 To prepare the king prawns, remove the shells. With a small, sharp knife, slit each prawn lengthways from head to tail; go right to the bottom of the flesh but make sure you don't separate the two halves entirely. With the tip of the knife, remove the black vein along the back. Cut off the head, then open the prawns out like a butterfly and skewer each one from head to tail.

2 Make a marinade by mixing together the lemon juice and turmeric with some salt and pepper. Rub this all over the skewered prawns and set them aside while you cook the filling.

3 Heat the oil in a frying pan over a medium heat and cook the chilli and garlic for 1 minute, then add the green pepper and onion and continue to cook for about about 5 minutes until the onions are soft and translucent. Stir in the cumin and ground coriander and cook for a further minute. Add the chopped tomato and turn the mixture out into a flat dish to cool.

4 Preheat the oven to 140°C/275°F/gas 1. When the pepper and onion mixture is cool, mix in the chopped prawns and all the remaining ingredients, and season to taste.

5 Place each skewered king prawn on a piece of aluminium foil and spread the spiced prawn mixture on each one, covering evenly. Fold each prawn lightly in foil to make a parcel. Measure 150ml (¼ pint) water in a jug and rub the reserved lemon skin between your fingers in the water to extract as much flavour from the rind as possible.

6 Take a baking tray and sprinkle the lemon liquid on the bottom, then place the prawns in their foil parcels on top and cook for 12–15 minutes. Check one parcel to ensure that the king prawn is cooked – the parcels may need a few minutes more in the oven. Serve with an extra spritz of lemon juice. Enjoy the prawns with either some rice or crusty bread.

SERVES 2

3–4 large uncooked king prawns, shell on
½–1 unwaxed lemon, juice extracted and skins reserved, plus extra juice to serve
½ tsp turmeric
1 tbsp rapeseed oil or vegetable oil
1–2 green chilli, seeds removed if liked, finely chopped
3 large cloves garlic, crushed
½ green pepper, cut into small dice
1 onion, finely chopped
1 tsp crushed cumin seeds
1 tsp ground coriander
1 tomato, skinned, de-seeded and chopped
15–20 cooked and peeled medium prawns, finely chopped
1 tbsp chopped fresh coriander
1 hard-boiled egg, white only, chopped
½ tsp lime juice
salt and freshly ground black pepper

This simple crab cake recipe works best with a combination of white and brown crab meat – but if you want to create a visually dazzling dish then tip the balance even further in favour of the white meat. This is derived from a classic dish, but I've put my own spin on it – I'm sure the traditionalists will complain…

Cyrus's

CRAB & POTATO CAKE WITH MUSTARD & CUMIN

1 For this recipe it's particularly handy to have all the ingredients prepared and in little bowls or ramekins, so that everything is to hand once cooking is underway. Heat the oil in a wok until nearly at smoking point – watch it carefully – and then ensure the heat is medium. Toss in the mustard seeds and cover loosely with a lid, so that the mustard seeds are contained when they start to pop.

2 When the seeds start to release a nutty aroma and the popping reduces, add the dried white lentils or yellow split peas and stir with a wooden spoon for a few seconds. They should change colour slightly and at that point add the cumin seeds, stir for a very few seconds, then add the ginger, chilli, shallots and asafoetida. Cook the mixture for 5 minutes or so, stirring often, until the shallots are translucent and soft.

3 Add the coconut and cook for a couple of minutes. The coconut should toast a little, and there should be very little liquid in the wok. Add the diced tomato and both crab meats, and mix well, cooking until the mixture is heated through. Finally add the coriander and some salt, and transfer to a bowl to cool.

4 Cook the potatoes in boiling salted water until soft. Drain them in a colander and return them to the pan on the heat for 1–2 minutes to dry out. Mash them, with a potato ricer if you have one, and season with a little salt and some pepper to taste. Mix in the shredded curry leaves, if using.

5 There are two ways to make the fishcakes: either mix together the mashed potato and crab mix; or shape some potato on your palm, place some crab filling, and add more potato to seal. Choose your method and make the fishcakes to your preferred size.

SERVES 4 AS A MAIN,
MORE AS A STARTER OR CANAPÉ

1–2 tbsp pure coconut oil, sunflower oil or rapeseed oil
½ tsp black mustard seeds
½ tsp dried white lentils, or yellow split peas
½ tsp cumin seeds
1 tbsp finely chopped or grated fresh root ginger
1 tbsp chopped fresh green chilli
6 baby red shallots, finely chopped (or 2 small red onions)
¼ tsp asafoetida (optional)
2 tbsp freshly grated coconut (or use 2 heaped tbsp desiccated coconut, soaked for 30 minutes in 50ml/2fl oz warm water)
1 tbsp diced fresh tomato
250g (9oz) fresh white crab meat
1 tbsp fresh brown crab meat
1 heaped tbsp chopped fresh coriander
3 large floury potatoes, peeled and cut into chunks
2–3 curry leaves, shredded (optional)
plain flour, to dust
2 eggs, beaten
200g (7oz) breadcrumbs, rice flour or medium semolina
rapeseed oil or vegetable oil, for shallow frying
juice of 1 lime, to drizzle
salt and freshly ground black pepper

6 Pat the fishcakes with a little flour, dip them briefly in the beaten egg and finally into the breadcrumbs, rice flour or semolina. If you have the time to spare, put them into the fridge for half an hour to firm up.

7 Heat a large non-stick frying pan, add a good splash of oil and fry the fishcakes for a few minutes on each side, until they are browned and warmed through; you may need to work in batches to avoid overcrowding the pan. Drain on kitchen paper and spritz with a little lime juice before serving. Serve with a little mayonnaise or perhaps with some Coriander Coalishlaw (see page 191).

The respect that Tony and I have for the cockles pickers of the Gower peninsula is unconditional. We spent a morning working with them and learnt so much – so I would like to dedicate this recipe to the amazing local folk who harvest these tiny pots of delicious golden meat. My recipe is as simple as simple can be, but do try to get the best smoked paprika and some good garlic; it really does make all the difference. Enjoy every morsel with some good crusty bread.

Cyrus's

COCKLES WITH SMOKED PAPRIKA & CORIANDER

1 In a small bowl, mix together well all of the ingredients for the butter, then set aside at room temperature

2 Rinse the cockles or mussels in a few changes of cold water to get rid of any grit, and drain thoroughly. Put them in a casserole pan with a tight-fitting lid and add the white wine, cover and cook on a high heat for 5 minutes, shaking the pan frequently. Take care not to overcook them, but check that most shells have opened.

3 With a slotted spoon, transfer all of the cockles or mussels to another bowl, retaining the juices in the hot pan. Over a high heat, reduce the juices to 1–2 tablespoons. Meanwhile, discard any cockles or mussels that did not open, and set aside a few that did open. From the remaining opened shells, remove the meat and put into a bowl.

4 Add the reduced juices to the butter and mix well. Heat a frying pan over a medium heat, add half of the butter mixture and the cockles or mussels, and toss for a few minutes. Add some more butter and toss for 1 minute more; ensure all are piping hot before removing from the heat. Serve over some greens, or inside a hollowed-out crusty white roll, and garnish with coriander and a few cockles or mussels in the shells.

SERVES 4 AS A STARTER, 2 FOR LUNCH
1kg (2lb 4oz) uncooked cockles
   or mussels in the shell
60ml (2¼fl oz) white wine
a few sprigs of coriander,
   to garnish

FOR THE BUTTER
3 tbsp lightly salted butter,
   softened
2 small garlic cloves, grated
1 tbsp lime juice
½ tsp smoked paprika
1 tbsp chopped fresh coriander
freshly ground black pepper

Tony's
COCKLE
PĪCKĪNG
WALES

When I was little, my family was quite poor. My mum had to be very imaginative, sometimes with quite limited ingredients. For instance, she used to make a salmon curry-stew from the heads and bones, something the fishmonger would probably throw away. We even sucked the marrow out of the larger spine bones. We ate crab and mussels too as well as a curry Mum made from smoked cod's roe, and we also had cockles from time to time.

Sometimes we would find fresh cockles, but we usually had them pickled. The cockles are boiled, then seasoned with malt vinegar and white pepper. These are the traditional British cockles sold at seaside stalls and in sea-front chippies: eaten from a small container with a little plastic two-pronged fork. Sadly, most of the fresh cockles gathered from our shores are now shipped to France, Holland and Spain (as are oysters, langoustines and scallops). Apart from in Wales, of course, where a traditional Welsh breakfast is cockles, laverbread (a local seaweed, known in Japan as *nori*), and bacon.

The dominant vinegar flavour may be traditional, but I like to play around with the sweetness of cockles – and of other bivalves, even prawns – and cook them with perhaps lime or lemon juice instead of vinegar, and also give them a bit of a

bite with some chilli. Ginger would be good too, as would capers. You could also use them to make a pasta sauce, Italian style.

We visited the Gower peninsula in Wales to see cockles being harvested. I don't envy those boys gathering the cockles from the mud (into which I nearly fell, tweed two-piece kilt and all). It's a really hard life, getting up and out for four in the morning, in all weathers, for less than 50p per kilo. There are 30 families involved in the Gower organisation, many of them fourth generation.

We cooked a cockle stew afterwards, using smoked paprika and some fresh coriander. It was delicious! And you can either serve them in their shells for a special meal (see page 86), or if you want to try a twist on this you could even shell them; the sweet spiced meat would make an amazing filling for a crusty bread roll.

And as if spicing up cockles wasn't enough, when in Hastings we even spiced up that favourite British seaside takeaway, fish and chips with mushy peas (see pages 62 and 184 for our recipes). Cyrus marinated white fish with turmeric, cumin, coriander and chilli powder before he battered and fried it. The chips were fried conventionally, but then he sprinkled them with chilli and cumin for a little lift. I added my bit with spiced mushy peas, which were spiked with tamarind instead of vinegar, and made unctuous with butter, like the best mashed potato. When we served them up to the hungry locals we suspected the fish might not be the only thing to get battered, but thankfully the bevy of bikers who tasted our spicy take on their favourite dish gave us the thumbs up!

CHĪCKEN

& POULTRY

An old standard, you can't go far wrong with chicken liver parfait. Here, we've spiced it up by adding a ginger kick. The fiery sweetness of the preserved ginger means that you don't need to serve this with a chutney on the side – so it's brilliant for taking on picnics. You can replace the ginger with cognac-soaked sultanas, if you fancy something a bit different.

Tony's

CHICKEN LIVER PARFAIT WITH GINGER PUNCH

1 Preheat the oven to 150°C/300°F/gas 2. Line a terrine dish, or a 600ml (1 pint) casserole dish, with the bacon rashers so that the slices only just overlap. Grease a piece of aluminium foil that will cover the dish.

2 Pour one tablespoon of the melted butter into a frying pan and cook the onion until softened but not browned. Add a splash of water if the pan looks dry. Meanwhile, in a separate pan, heat another tablespoon of the melted butter and cook the chicken livers and garlic for a few minutes on each side, or until lightly browned but still pink in the centre. Set the livers aside and discard the garlic.

3 Add the whisky and port to the onions, then the bay leaf and thyme, and boil until the liquid has reduced by two-thirds. Strain the whisky and port liquid onto the warm chicken livers. Discard the onions and herbs. Put a kettle on to boil.

4 Place the livers and liquid into a food-processor and purée. While the mixture is being processed, slowly add two-thirds of the remaining melted butter – it's important to do this slowly, otherwise the mixture will curdle.

5 When all of the butter has been incorporated, stir in the nutmeg and cinnamon and pass the mixture through a sieve into a jug. Pour into the lined terrine or casserole dish and cover the dish with the greased foil.

6 Place a large roasting tin in the oven and place the terrine into it. Carefully pour boiling water into the roasting tin to come halfway up the sides of the terrine dish. Cook for 40 minutes or until just set.

7 Remove the terrine from the oven, sprinkle the stem ginger on top and pour over the remaining melted butter. Set the parfait aside to cool. Once cool, place in the fridge and leave overnight. To serve, slice the parfait and serve with lettuce leaves and crisp sourdough toast.

SERVES 4–6 AS A STARTER
6 rashers streaky bacon
300g (10½oz) butter, melted, plus extra for greasing
1 onion, sliced
400g (14oz) chicken livers, trimmed, rinsed and cleaned
8 garlic cloves
100ml (3½fl oz) whisky
100ml (3½fl oz) ruby port
1 bay leaf
sprig of thyme
pinch of grated nutmeg
pinch ground cinnamon
100g (4oz) preserved stem ginger in syrup, drained and finely chopped

The Coronation chicken usually found in Britain is often sweeter and jammier than the Indian creation, but this recipe brings flavours that are truly resplendent. It uses a whole chicken, much more than is needed for a few sandwiches, but enough for six as a filling salad; any left over can fill sandwiches. If you want to use up some leftover roast chicken, braise it gently as below before mixing it with the mayonnaise dressing.

Cyrus's

BOMBAY CORONATION CHICKEN

1 Heat 1 tbsp of the oil in a frying pan, and cook the cinnamon or cassia bark, peppercorns and bay leaves over a medium heat for a few minutes.

2 Add the chopped onions and some salt, reduce the heat and cook until softened. Add the ginger and the curry powder, continue to cook for a minute, then add the Worcestershire sauce, wine and chopped tomato, and bring to the boil. Boil for a minute, then add the mango chutney and 200ml (7fl oz) of water. Mix well, then switch off the heat and set aside.

3 Heat the remaining oil in a casserole dish. Add the chicken pieces and brown on all sides. Pour the onion mixture over the chicken, ensuring there is at least 1cm (½in) of liquid in the pan (if not, add a splash of water). Cover with a tight lid and simmer on a low heat for at least 45 minutes until the chicken is cooked. Check every now and then throughout cooking and top up with more water if required.

4 Remove the chicken pieces from the cooking liquid and transfer to a dish. Reserve the cooking liquid. Shred the chicken with forks and cool.

5 You will need 5 tablespoons of cooking liquid to flavour the mayonnaise dressing; if there is much more than that remaining in the casserole dish, boil it over a high heat to reduce it. Remove the cinnamon or cassia bark, peppercorns and bay leaves and purée the remaining mixture.

6 Heat a frying pan over a low heat and toast the curry powder, stirring continuously, until it releases a fabulous aroma that indicates it is ready.

7 Mix the toasted curry powder into the mayonnaise, then add the green chilli and coriander. Gradually mix 5 tablespoons of the puréed cooking liquid, then mix in the yoghurt, apricots and almonds. Season to taste.

8 Mix the shredded chicken with the mayonnaise dressing. To serve the chicken as a salad, set it on a bed of mixed lettuce or cold steamed rice.

SERVES 6 AS A SALAD

3 tbsp sunflower oil
7.5cm (3in) piece cinnamon stick or cassia bark, broken in half
6 black peppercorns
3 small bay leaves
2 red onions, chopped
7.5cm (3in) piece fresh root ginger, cut into small pieces
1 tsp curry powder
1 tsp Worcestershire sauce
150ml (5fl oz) white wine
1½ tomatoes, chopped
1 heaped tbsp sweet mango chutney
1–1.5kg (2lb 4oz–3lb) whole chicken, with skin, jointed into 2 legs and 2 breasts and remaining carcass cut into 3–4 pieces, patted dry and seasoned

FOR THE MAYONNAISE DRESSING

2 tsp curry powder
150–200g (5–7oz) good-quality mayonnaise, depending on the quantity of chicken used
1–2 fresh green chillies, seeds removed if liked, finely chopped
1 tbsp chopped fresh coriander
1 heaped tbsp Greek-style yoghurt
5 soft dried apricots, diced small
12 almonds, chopped
salt and freshly ground black pepper

This is such an easy dish to put together, but the thing I love the most about it is that it's a real mix and match recipe – if you want something a bit more special you can swap the meat for whole quails, pigeon breasts or some guinea fowl; any gamey meat you fancy.

Tony's

TANDOORI-ROASTED CHICKEN

1 With a sharp knife or fork, pierce the flesh of the chicken thighs in a few places to help the marinade get into the meat. Mix together the ingredients for the first marinade and rub well into the chicken. Cover and leave to marinate in the fridge for 4–6 hours (but if you are short of time you can proceed with the next step straight away).

2 In a large bowl, mix together all the ingredients for the second marinade and rub well into the chicken. Cover and leave to marinate in the fridge overnight (again, if you are short of time you can proceed with the next step straight away).

3 Preheat the oven to 180°C/350°F/gas 4. Put the chicken in a casserole dish and cover with a lid. Cook in the preheated oven for 45 minutes, basting twice during cooking with the juices. Uncover the casserole dish and cook for a further 15 minutes, or until the chicken is tender.

4 Remove the dish from the oven, season to taste and stir in the coriander, then cover and rest the chicken for 5 minutes. Squeeze over the lemon juice, if using, and serve hot, with a red onion salad and some mint chutney.

SERVES 4–6

6–8 chicken thighs on the bone, skin removed
2 large handfuls of chopped fresh coriander, to garnish
juice of 1 lemon (optional)

FOR THE FIRST MARINADE

2 tbsp grated fresh root ginger
1 tbsp garlic purée
1 tbsp rapeseed oil or vegetable oil

FOR THE SECOND MARINADE

100g (4oz) natural yoghurt
1 tsp ground cardamom (about 24 cardamom pods, seeds finely ground)
½ tsp ground cinnamon
1 tsp garam masala
¼ tsp ground mace
50ml (2fl oz) double cream
½ tsp saffron strands, soaked in 1 tbsp warm milk (optional)
salt

An all-time favourite for the kids, this. Watching movies with a big plate of spiced wings, they'll be happy for hours! The amazing by-product of this recipe, though, is the spice mix – great on chips, amazing on baked potatoes, and if you're grilling on the barbecue just sprinkle some of this over your meat. Stunning. Serve them up with the Peanut and Mint Slaw on page 190 and tuck in.

Tony

COLONEL SĪNGH'S SPĪCED WĪNGS

1 First make the cure for the chicken wings. Cut the head of garlic several times across the width and discard as much of the papery skin as you can. Put the garlic in a large shallow dish and add all of the remaining cure ingredients. With a pestle, gently bruise the mixture to release the flavours. Add the chicken wings and massage the cure into them. Cover and refrigerate for at least 6 hours, overnight if possible.

2 When ready to cook the chicken, preheat the oven to 150°C/300°F/gas 2. Remove the chicken wings from the fridge, wipe off the cure with kitchen paper and pat as dry as possible. Place them in a deep ovenproof pot with a tightly fitting lid, add the cinnamon sticks and enough oil to submerge the meat. Cover with the lid and cook in the preheated oven for 3 hours; there is no need to disturb the dish during this time.

3 Remove the pot from the oven and leave the chicken to cool in the oil while you make the dusting. The chicken will need one final quick cook in the oven before it is ready to eat, so don't turn the oven off; instead, increase the temperature to 220°C/425°F/gas 7.

4 Whizz together the ingredients for the dusting in a mini chopper or food-processor and set aside.

5 When the chicken wings have cooled, line a dish with a double layer of kitchen paper. With a slotted spoon, remove the chicken wings from the oil (carefully as they will be very tender) and place on the kitchen paper for a few minutes so that it soaks up some of the oil. Carefully transfer the wings to a roasting tin, and roast in the preheated oven for 12 minutes or so or until crispy.

6 Remove the wings from the oven and pat with kitchen paper again. Shake over the dusting and serve, allowing three chicken wings per person. Serve any extra dusting alongside in case you want to add even more!

SERVES 4
12 chicken wings, skin on
2 x 4cm (1½in) cinnamon sticks
500–700ml (17fl oz–1¼ pints) vegetable oil or rapeseed oil

FOR THE CURE
1 head of garlic
1 bunch fresh thyme, roughly chopped
3 tbsp grated ginger, including its skin
6 dried red chillies, roughly broken
4 tbsp sea salt

FOR COLONEL SĪNGH'S DUSTING
3 tsp rubbed sage or crushed dried sage
1 tbsp garlic powder (optional)
1 tbsp vegetable bouillon powder
1 tsp chilli powder
1 tsp dried thyme
½ tbsp sea salt

Cyrus's
SPĪCE
FOCUS
CHĪLLĪ

The chilli pepper puts heat into cooking around the world. Christopher Columbus found chillies in the Americas in 1492 (along with their relations, tomato, potato and tobacco), and because they were hot and spicy, like peppercorns, he named them *pimiento*, or pepper. After this, chillies took only about 50 years to spread everywhere. They were not only easy to grow, but could replace the expensive peppercorns. India took enthusiastically to the chilli: until its arrival, heat in curries had been supplied only by peppercorns, mustard and ginger.

There are many species of chilli, which are used fresh, green or red, dried whole, or dried and ground. They vary in heat, and I learned very early on how to buy them. Mum would take me to the market and point out the little Scud missiles (far too hot), the thin longer ones (not too hot) and then the broad ones (the least hot). There is still some truth in this: generally, smaller chillies are more lethal, so I tend to use larger chillies in my recipes. As Parsees don't eat their food very hot, we usually use Kashmiri chillies, which are thick, long, mild, and very crinkly when dried.

The heat in chillies comes from a substance called capsaicin. When eaten, the brain thinks the body is being attacked: as protection, the heart rate rises, perspiration increases and endorphins are released. These natural painkillers are associated with pleasure, so it could be true that eating chillies can be addictive! (Capsicum plasters, utilising capsaicin, are still used for topical pain relief in Asia.) Incidentally, if I eat something too chilli hot, I always prefer to drink milk or yoghurt to cool my mouth, not water or alcohol, as some people tend to do.

But chillies aren't just hot, they can be extremely flavourful as well. My favourite Kashmiri chilli adds a fruity, sweet and earthy note to many dishes, as well as colour, and along with other chillies can add a spicy sparkle to traditional British vegetable soups, shepherd's pies, baked beans, mash, Yorkshire puds, even breakfast! Chilli spiciness with sweet things – chocolate, for instance – is really interesting, and the Morris dancers we met while filming in Hastings seemed to enjoy our ice cream sprinkled with a little chilli powder and cinnamon!

Chillies are made into many different types of products: dried they become chilli powder, cayenne pepper, paprika (plain or smoked) or chilli flakes. They are made into sauces like Tabasco and the Portuguese piri-piri, and in India they are an essential part of many curry powders and masalas. Versatile, exciting and taste-enhancing, I think chillies are a real superfood.

This is a very simple dish to make and is a great way of using up leftover vegetables; just throw in anything that you have to hand. I would personally not remove the seeds of the chillies as they add more flavour, but please do so if you are a little scared. This recipe works best if the oil is really hot and starting to smoke before you add the chicken.

Cyrus's

EASY PEASY CHILLI CHICKEN

1 To make the marinade, tip the garlic and chillies into a mini food-processor and blend to a paste. Mix in the remaining marinade ingredients. In a large bowl, mix the marinade and the chicken strips so that all the pieces are well coated. You can cook the chicken immediately, but if time allows, cover the bowl and set aside for 30 minutes. It is important for the chicken to have a slightly sticky texture, so if it is a little dry add some more cornflour.

2 Heat the oil in a large, heavy-bottomed pan or wok over a high heat. Place a colander over a bowl and keep it nearby. Add the chicken piece by piece into the oil – the pieces will start to stick together, so keep separating them so that they fry individually. Cook uncovered, stirring often, for about 6-8 minutes until the chicken is cooked through and starting to colour well. As soon as the chicken is ready remove it from the pan with a slotted spoon and set aside on some kitchen paper.

3 Add the spring onion, pepper and additional vegetables to the pan and cook uncovered, stirring, for 2–3 minutes. Return the chicken to the pan and warm through. Taste and add any seasoning as required, and serve.

SERVES 4

FOR THE MARINADE
4 garlic cloves
2 fresh green chillies,
    seeds removed if liked,
    roughly chopped
1 tbsp red wine vinegar
1 tbsp dark soy sauce
1 tbsp chilli sauce
1 heaped tbsp cornflour,
    mixed to a paste with
    1 tbsp cold water
1 tsp salt

FOR THE CHICKEN
800g (1lb 14oz) skinless chicken
    thigh fillets, cut into strips
    1–2cm (½–¾in) thick
6–8 tbsp vegetable oil or
    rapeseed oil
1 bunch spring onions,
    cut into 3cm (1¼in) pieces
1–2 red or yellow peppers, seeds
    removed, thinly sliced
a handful of vegetables, such as
    baby corn and celery, stringed
    and sliced (optional)
salt and freshly ground black
    pepper

A simple dish, great for winter evenings when you want something warming but not too heavy. And, even better, it's good and cheap, as you can get good-quality chicken thighs without breaking the bank. If you want to make this a bit more special, try it with wild mushrooms.

Tony's

POT-ROASTED THIGHS WITH MUSHROOMS & MASH

1 First make the masala paste. Heat the oil in a pan on a medium heat, add the onions and cook for 10 minutes until soft and golden.

2 Add the cumin seeds and the puréed garlic and ginger, and cook for a further 1–2 minutes until they release their aromas. Mix in all of the spices except the amchoor, and cook on a low heat until the oil starts separating from the mix.

3 Add the tomatoes and simmer on a low heat for 20–30 minutes until reduced to a thick, rich consistency. If the masala starts to stick to the bottom of the pan, add a splash of water but continue to cook gently to reduce again – this slow cooking is very important to develop flavours. Remove the pan from the heat, stir in the amchoor, if using, and season with salt to taste. The paste can last for up to 5 days in the fridge.

4 When ready to cook the rest of the dish, start with the potatoes. Preheat the oven to minimum. Cook the potatoes in boiling salted water until tender, then drain thoroughly. Return them to the pan, add the butter and cream and mash together over a low heat. Season to taste and stir in the chives. Keep warm in the oven.

5 To cook the mushrooms, heat a large pan over a medium heat, add the butter and let it melt, then add the mushrooms and gently cook for 5–6 minutes or until golden and softened. Meanwhile, boil the peas until just tender and drain thoroughly. Add the peas to the mushrooms, drizzle with a little truffle oil and season to taste. Keep warm in the oven.

6 To cook the chicken, heat 1 tbsp of the 50ml (2fl oz) oil in a large frying pan over medium-high heat. Season the chicken thighs, add them to the pan and cook on all sides for about 5 minutes until browned. If your pan isn't big enough to take all the pieces in a single layer, brown them in batches. Put the chicken onto a large plate, spoon over the masala and,

SERVES 4–6

50ml (2fl oz) rapeseed oil
   or vegetable oil
1.2kg (2lb 10oz) chicken thighs
   (8–10 chicken thighs) on
   the bone, skin removed
100g (4oz) masala paste
   (see below)
1 small carrot, roughly chopped
1 small onion, roughly chopped
1 small leek, roughly chopped
1 stick celery, roughly chopped
1 bulb garlic (about 50g/2oz),
   cut in half through the equator
a few sprigs fresh thyme
75g (3oz) butter, diced and
   chilled
salt and freshly ground black
   pepper

FOR THE MASALA PASTE

4 tbsp rapeseed oil or
   vegetable oil
2 onions, finely chopped
1½ tsp cumin seeds
10 garlic cloves, puréed
20g (¾oz) ginger purée
4 tsp ground coriander
4 tsp chilli powder
1 tsp turmeric
2½ tsp garam masala
1 x 400g (14oz) tin chopped
   tomatoes
1 tsp amchoor powder (optional)

Continues overleaf

when the chicken pieces are cool enough to handle, rub the paste
all over them.

7 Heat the remaining oil in a large heavy-based saucepan or casserole
dish with a lid over a medium heat. Add the vegetables and garlic and
fry for 5 minutes until golden. Add the masala-rubbed chicken and any
juices from the plate, and throw in the thyme. Add 750ml (1 pint 7fl oz)
water and bring to a simmer, cover with a lid and simmer gently for
45 minutes or until the chicken is tender.

8 Remove the chicken pieces from the pan and keep them warm in the
oven. Strain the cooking liquor through a sieve into a clean pan (discard
the vegetables or reserve to stir back into the sauce before serving).
Boil to reduce to roughly 250ml (9fl oz), then reduce the heat to low and
whisk in the butter one cube at a time until you have a smooth, glossy
and thick sauce. Do not allow the sauce to boil once you have added
the butter. If you want a more homely sauce, then return the still-warm
vegetables – but not the garlic or thyme – to the sauce. To serve, put
mash in the centre of individual plates, with the chicken on top.
Spoon the mushrooms and peas around, pour the sauce over and
around, and serve.

FOR THE POTATOES

900g (2lb) potatoes,
   peeled and cut into chunks
75g (3oz) butter
75ml (2¾fl oz) double cream
25g (1oz) chopped chives

FOR THE MUSHROOMS

25g (1oz) butter
225g (8oz) chestnut mushrooms
   (or use fresh morels if you
   prefer), cut into 1cm (½in)
   thick slices or left whole if
   very small
200g (7oz) frozen peas,
   defrosted (or use fresh
   if available)
1 tsp light truffle oil, or to taste

I simply love coriander, and seeing how popular it is becoming I thought it best to devote a recipe to its wonderful flavours, which leave a delicious, lingering note on the palate. This comes from an old Indian classic, but I've adapted it to make a simple and practical way of spicing up chicken breasts.

Cyrus's
CHICKEN BREAST MADE SEXY

1 Pat the chicken breasts clean and dry. With a pestle and mortar, crush the coriander seeds well. Add the chilli, garlic, lime juice, oil and a generous amount of salt, and pound well to form a coarse masala rub.

2 Rub this masala well into the chicken, then cover and place in the fridge for a few hours if time permits. When ready to cook, remove the chicken from the fridge and preheat the oven and a roasting tin to 200°C/400°F/gas 6.

3 Meanwhile, start the sauce. Heat the oil in a saucepan, add the green chillies and ginger, and cook until the chillies change colour. Add the onions and continue cooking over a medium heat until they are soft and translucent but not browned.

4 Put the cumin, turmeric, chilli powder and ground coriander in a bowl, and stir in 200ml (7fl oz) of water. Add this to the onions, then continue cooking until the liquid nearly dries up. Add the tomatoes and cover loosely, and continue cooking, stirring regularly, until the tomatoes are cooked and you have a lovely sauce. Set aside.

5 Set the chicken breasts skin-side up in the hot roasting tin and roast in the preheated oven for 10 minutes, then reduce the temperature to 140°C/275°F/gas 1. Continue roasting for 10 minutes, then reduce the heat to minimum and continue roasting for 10 minutes. Switch off the oven and leave the chicken inside to rest for 10 minutes.

6 Add the chopped coriander to the sauce and season to taste. Place the rested chicken breasts in the sauce, pour in the juices from the roasting tin to make a gravy and cover. Simmer for a minute or two if the chicken was fully cooked in the oven; if not, simmer until fully cooked. Serve with hot crusty bread or steamed rice.

SERVES 4

4 large chicken breasts, skin on
2 tsp coriander seeds
1 tsp red chilli flakes or crushed dried red chilli
2 garlic cloves
1 tbsp lime juice
1 tbsp sunflower oil or rapeseed oil
sea salt

FOR THE SAUCE

2 tbsp sunflower oil
2 fresh green chillies, deseeded if liked, cut in four lengthways
7.5cm (3in) piece of fresh root ginger, peeled and finely chopped (the discarded skin can be left to dry and then added to a cup of tea)
2 red onions, cut in half and thinly sliced
1 tsp ground cumin
½ tsp turmeric
½ tsp chilli powder
½ tsp ground coriander
1 x 400g (14oz) tin chopped tomatoes or 500g (1lb 2oz) fresh tomatoes, chopped
2 heaped tbsp chopped fresh coriander

I love the sweetness and woody vanilla flavour in this dish, which works really well with the rosemary in the polenta and the little kick of heat from the chilli. All together, truly scrumptious.

Tony's

ROAST MAPLE & CHILLI CHICKEN WITH POLENTA

1 Put all the marinade ingredients into a pan and bring to the boil on a medium heat, stirring constantly. Continue boiling until the mixture thickens to a syrupy consistency. Leave to cool, then pour the marinade over the chicken breast fillets and refrigerate until you are ready to cook them.

2 Preheat the oven to 200°C/400°F/gas 6. Prepare the roasting vegetables: cut the onions into large dice and slice the peppers and the carrots into batons. Chop the celeriac and aubergine into 5cm (2in) cubes and thickly slice the leek and parsnip. Assemble all of the vegetables and the garlic in a large bowl, add the oil and mix well. Line the bottom of a large baking sheet with baking parchment, tip in the vegetables and roast in the preheated oven for 10 minutes. Meanwhile, put the prepared chicken on another baking sheet. When the vegetables have been roasting for 10 minutes, put the baking sheet with the chicken into the oven and continue roasting for 30 minutes.

3 To cook the polenta, melt the butter in a large saucepan, add the shallots and cook on a medium heat for about 5 minutes until softened. Add the garlic and cook for a further minute, then mix in the rosemary. Add the vegetable stock and bring to the boil, then sprinkle in the polenta and Parmesan. Use a balloon whisk to ensure no lumps remain, return to the boil and then cook on a low heat for around 5 minutes, stirring frequently, until the mixture is smooth and no longer grainy.

4 To serve, spoon some polenta into the centre of the plates, add the vegetables around and sit the chicken on top. Garnish each plate with thyme leaves.

SERVES 6
6 x 220g (8oz) chicken breast fillets
salt and freshly ground black pepper

FOR THE MARINADE
150ml (¼ pint) maple syrup
3 fresh green finger chillies
1 tbsp chopped fresh thyme leaves, plus extra to garnish
2 tbsp white wine vinegar
1 tbsp clear honey

FOR THE ROASTED VEGETABLES
2 red onions
1 red pepper
1 yellow pepper
1 carrot, peeled
1 small celeriac
1 large aubergine
1 leek
1 parsnip, peeled
2 garlic cloves, crushed
30–50ml (1–2fl oz) peanut oil or sunflower oil

FOR THE POLENTA
50g (2oz) butter
50g (2oz) shallots, chopped
1 garlic clove, crushed
15g (½oz) rosemary, chopped
860ml (1½ pints) vegetable stock
175g (6oz) fine polenta
50g (2oz) Parmesan, grated

This chicken is flavoured with a combination I have liked very much since childhood. I had acute asthma, and when the coughing fits got too heavy my parents would make me a juice of ginger blended with turmeric, honey and cinnamon. It worked like a dream, and to this day I swear by it. I tried roasting chicken with the mixture one day, adding some other touches – it was fantastic. To serve this with Tony's roasties, you'll need two ovens; the cooking temperatures are different.

Cyrus's

HONEY-ROASTED CHICKEN WITH OUTSTANDING ROASTIES

1 In a blender or mini food-processor, blitz together all of the marinade ingredients to a fine paste. Taste and adjust the seasoning if liked.

2 Pat the chicken dry with kitchen paper. Put it in a dish and rub the marinade all over it and if time allows let it rest for an hour or so in the fridge. Preheat an oven to 180°C/350°F/gas 4.

3 Put the chicken in a roasting tin and baste with any excess marinade, reserving anything left over. Put the roasting tin in the oven and cook for 1 hour. You need to keep an eye on it for the first 10–15 minutes – the honey in the marinade will burn, so allow the chicken to brown in these first few minutes, and then cover it loosely with aluminium foil. Baste the chicken a few times during cooking, adding some of the reserved marinade if it starts to look dry.

4 To cook the potatoes, preheat an oven to 220°C/425°F/gas 7. Put the prepared potatoes in a pan of salted water, bring to the boil, then reduce the heat and simmer for about 7 minutes till only just underdone. Meanwhile, pour the oil into a large roasting tin and put into the oven for 5 minutes until hot.

5 Drain the potatoes well. Cover the pan and shake the potatoes about – you want to bash up their edges but not break them up. Gently transfer them to the hot roasting tin, turn them about in the hot oil and sprinkle with salt. Roast on the top shelf for 30 minutes, then turn them over and roast for a further 20–30 minutes or until crisp and golden.

6 After the chicken has been roasting for 1 hour, check whether it is cooked. (The meat is cooked when a thin skewer or a thick needle inserted in the thigh joint produces a clear liquid.) Transfer to a serving dish, cover the chicken with foil and allow it to rest for 5 minutes before you carve it.

SERVES 4
1.2kg (2lb 10oz) chicken

FOR THE MARINADE
6 tbsp honey
50g (2oz) fresh root ginger, chopped
1 tsp turmeric
1 tsp ground cinnamon
3 tbsp light soy sauce
2 tbsp lime juice
3 tbsp cold-pressed rapeseed or olive oil
salt and freshly ground black pepper

FOR THE ROASTIES
1–1.2kg (2lb 4oz–2lb 10oz) floury potatoes, peeled and cut roughly into 5cm (2in) chunks
100ml (3½fl oz) rapeseed oil or vegetable oil
2 tsp dried sage
1 tsp chilli powder
1 tsp vegetable bouillon powder
¼ tsp garlic powder (optional)

Continues overleaf

7 Meanwhile, strain the liquid from the roasting tin into a small pan, adjust the seasoning to taste and keep warm.

8 Mix together the sage, chilli powder, bouillon powder and garlic powder if using, to make a spice mix. Remove the potatoes from the oven, set them on a plate lined with kitchen paper, and sprinkle over the spice mix.

9 Joint and serve the roast chicken alongside the roast potatoes, drizzled with the juices from the roasting pan.

These chicken escalopes are the perfect marriage of oriental and Mediterranean tastes. The recipe is a little fiddly, but once you've prepared it you'll see how exciting the flavours are. If you want to take things a little further, add a dash of fish sauce and some chopped green chilli to the marinade.

Cyrus's
GINGER CHICKEN ESCALOPES

1 To prepare the mushrooms, heat the butter and 1 tbsp of the oil together in a frying pan over a medium-high heat, add the mushrooms and cook for 5–7 minutes until coloured and softened. Add the garlic and fry for a minute, then season with the oregano or mixed Italian herbs and some salt and pepper. Keep warm.

2 Heat the remaining oil in a pan over a medium-high heat, add the onion and cook for 10 minutes until softened.

3 To prepare the chicken, loosely wrap each breast in clingfilm and flatten with a meat mallet to about 1cm (½in) thick. In a shallow dish, mix together the ginger, garlic, soy sauce, Worcestershire sauce and oregano or mixed Italian herbs. Add 1 tablespoon of the oil and some pepper, then add the chicken breasts and rub the mixture all over.

4 When ready to cook, griddle or grill the bacon until crispy, then remove onto kitchen paper and keep warm.

5 Heat a large frying pan over a medium-high heat with a drizzle of the remaining oil. Add the chicken, holding back any excess marinade. Cook for 3–4 minutes on each side, or until cooked through and nicely browned, adding any extra marinade for the last 3 minutes or so of cooking (you can also add any liquid that has oozed from the cooked mushrooms at this point). Transfer the chicken to warm serving plates.

6 Pour the wine and sherry into the pan used to cook the chicken, bring to the boil and bubble for 1–2 minutes to reduce, scraping any browned bits off the bottom of the pan. Add the chicken stock and bring to a simmer, then stir in the cornflour and cook for 1 minute until thickened to a gravy; if it gets too thick, add a splash of boiling water. Top the chicken with the bacon and arrange the onions and mushrooms alongside. Pour over the sauce and serve with garlic bread.

SERVES 2

FOR THE MUSHROOMS
15g (½oz) butter
2 tbsp rapeseed oil or vegetable oil
200g (7oz) mushrooms, sliced ½cm (¼in) thick
1 garlic clove, finely chopped
½ tsp dried oregano or dried mixed Italian herbs
salt and freshly ground black pepper
1 onion, thinly sliced

FOR THE CHICKEN
2 boneless chicken breasts, skin removed
4cm (1½in) piece fresh root ginger, finely grated
2 garlic cloves, finely crushed
1 tbsp dark soy sauce
1 tsp Worcestershire sauce
2 tsp dried oregano or dried mixed Italian herbs
2 tbsp rapeseed oil or vegetable oil
6–8 rashers streaky bacon
100ml (3½fl oz) red wine
30ml (1¼fl oz) sherry
¼ chicken stock cube, dissolved in 100ml (3½fl oz) boiling water
1 tsp cornflour, mixed to a paste with 1–2 tbsp cold water
garlic bread, to serve

Tikkas are Indian dishes of small pieces of meat or vegetables marinated in a spice mixture. There are several variations to the original tikka recipe, and you can use your own imagination to create more interesting kebabs. This basic chicken tikka marinade can be used for various poultry meats. Here we use turkey breast, but if you were to try chicken instead, you could use leg meat too.

Cyrus's
TURKEY TIKKA

1 Cut the turkey into 3.5cm (1½in) cubes. Rub in the turmeric and some salt and pepper and set aside in the fridge while you make the marinade.

2 Spoon half of the yoghurt into a blender and add all of the remaining ingredients apart from the butter, then blend until smooth. Transfer the mixture to a bowl and whisk in the remaining yoghurt. Rub this mixture well into the turkey and refrigerate for at least 4 hours, or overnight if time permits.

3 If you like, you can thread the marinated turkey onto 8–10 metal skewers. To cook, place under a medium grill with a drip tray below, or chargrill on a medium barbecue; either way, cook the turkey for 5–7 minutes if in loose pieces (about 15 minutes if skewered), or until the juices run clear, repeatedly turning and basting with the melted butter for a juicy appearance.

NOTE: The turkey can also be cooked in the oven at 190°C/375°F/gas 5, but the result is not so pleasing.

SERVES 4–6
800g (1lb 14oz) boneless turkey
    breast, skin removed
1 tsp turmeric
salt and freshly ground black
    pepper

FOR THE MARINADE
150g (5oz) natural full-fat
    yoghurt
4cm (1½in) piece of fresh
    root ginger, peeled
4 garlic cloves
½ tsp ground cumin
½ tsp ground coriander
½ tsp chilli powder
1 tbsp lime juice
½ tsp garam masala
2 mild fresh green chillies
    (optional), seeds removed
    if liked, roughly chopped
2 tbsp sunflower oil or
    rapeseed oil
20g (¾oz) butter, melted
salt and ground white pepper

PORK, LAMB, BEEF

& OTHER MEAT

I made this recipe in a mad competition with our local Chinese restaurant. Me and some friends used to eat their ribs with a few bevvies when we had our card nights, and I boasted that I could make a better version. After a day of working hard in the kitchen I had the perfect recipe, but couldn't crack the batter. So, head held low, I admitted defeat and asked the restaurant for their secret ingredient – custard powder! You have got to try it, it is out of this world.

Tony's

SALT & CHILLI RIBS

1 Preheat the oven to 180°C/350°F/gas 4. Arrange the pork ribs in a single layer in an ovenproof dish. To create a braising liquor, put 600ml (1 pint) of water in a medium pan, add the bouillon powder, garlic purée, white wine, chilli bean sauce and char siu sauce, and bring to the boil.

2 Pour the braising liquor over the ribs, cover the dish with a double layer of aluminium foil, and cook in the oven for approximately 2¼ hours, basting a few times throughout.

3 Meanwhile, make the dry spice mix. Heat a small frying pan and dry-fry the white peppercorns, Sichuan pepper and star anise until they release their aroma. Crush them with a pestle and mortar, then mix with the remaining ingredients. Store in an airtight jar.

4 When the rib meat is soft yet still well attached to the bone, remove from the oven and leave to cool in the braising liquid. Once cool remove from the liquid to a tray to dry out. Discard the braising liquid.

5 If you have a deep fryer, heat the corn oil to 165–170°C (330–340°F), and mix together all the batter ingredients to a batter/paste. Ensure the ribs are dry, then cover them with the batter. Deep fry in batches for about 30 seconds or until golden brown and crispy. To pan-fry the ribs instead of deep frying, mix together all the batter ingredients except the sesame oil to create a dusting for the ribs – dust the ribs with this. Heat the vegetable or rapeseed oil in a large frying pan and fry the ribs in batches.

6 To make the garnish, finely dice the spring onions, chillies and peppers. Heat the oil in a frying pan and briefly sauté all the remaining garnish ingredients. As soon as the ribs and garnish are ready, mix them together in a large bowl. Sprinkle with the reserved dry spice mix to taste. Serve the ribs with extra dry spice mix alongside for sprinkling.

SERVES 4

1 kg (2lb 4oz) pork ribs
1 tbsp vegetable bouillon powder
1 tbsp garlic purée
300ml (½ pint) white wine
1 tbsp chilli bean sauce (toban)
½ jar char siu sauce
corn oil, if deep frying

FOR THE DRY SPICE MIX

½ tbsp white peppercorns
1 tbsp Sichuan pepper
4 star anise
3 tsp salt
1 tsp chilli flakes
1 tbsp five-spice powder
½ tbsp crushed black pepper
½ tbsp caster sugar
½ tbsp vegetable bouillon powder

FOR THE BATTER

2 tsp salt
1 tsp garlic purée
½ tsp chilli powder
6 tbsp custard powder
6 tsp plain flour
2 tbsp sesame oil, if deep frying
2 tbsp vegetable oil or rapeseed oil, if pan frying

FOR THE GARNISH

1 tbsp rapeseed oil or vegetable oil
8 spring onions
3 red chillies
½ red pepper, seeds removed
½ yellow pepper, seeds removed

The title is a nickname for Hibs, my football team, but the recipe itself actually comes from memories of a dish that my granny used to make me. She'd use a belly of lamb, chopped up and cooked with white cabbage until the meat fell off the bone and the cabbage melted in your mouth. This is my take on it using pork, but it'll work just as well with lamb if you can get hold of it.

Tony's
CABBAGE & RĪBS

1 Heat three tablespoons of the oil in a large deep pan that has a lid over a medium-high heat. Working in batches, add the ribs and cook until browned on all sides – about 5 minutes each batch. Set the batches aside on a plate as you cook the next. You will most likely need to add a little more oil for each batch.

2 When all the meat has been browned and removed from the pan, reduce the heat to low, heat the remaining oil in the pan and fry the onions until softened, adding a splash of the water to the pan and scraping to release any brown bits of meat stuck to the bottom.

3 Add the garlic and the dry spices and some salt, stir to combine, then pour in 200ml (7fl oz) water. Stir in the tinned tomatoes, ginger and green chillies and turn up the heat.

4 Add the ribs and stir to coat them in the sauce, then tip the cabbage over the top and cover with a tight-fitting lid. Cook at a steady simmer for 45 minutes–1 hour, until the meat falls off the bone and the cabbage is cooked. Check the pan from time to time and add a splash of water if the mixture starts to dry out. Serve with chapattis.

SERVES 6

6 tbsp rapeseed oil or vegetable oil
1.5kg (3lb) pork spare ribs, separated into individual ribs
2 onions (preferably Spanish onions), chopped
4 garlic cloves, crushed
1 tbsp ground turmeric
1 tbsp garam masala
1 tsp chilli powder
1 x 400g (14oz) tin chopped tomatoes
7.5cm (3in) piece fresh root ginger, chopped
3–4 small green chillies, bashed with a rolling pin
1 head white cabbage, cored, roughly chopped, then washed and drained
salt

Gammon and coriander seeds have a time-honoured partnership, and have long been used to preserve meat. Our visit to a cider barn in Somerset (see page 202) inspired us to add some additional flavours. Using both cider and apple juice, and adding a bite of red chilli to the flavour of the coriander seeds adds a real sparkle to this dish. Tony's Spiced Red Cabbage on page 186 and Green Chilli Mash on page 187 make a great combination.

Cyrus's

EXCEPTIONAL GAMMON WITH CIDER & CINNAMON

1 Soak the gammon in plenty of cold water in the fridge for at least 2 hours, or overnight. Drain well.

2 Place the gammon along with all the other gammon ingredients in a casserole dish. The liquid should cover the meat; if not, add a little water to just cover. Bring to the boil, then reduce the heat to low and simmer gently, partly covered with a lid, for 1¼ hours. Turn the gammon carefully in the liquid every 20 minutes or so.

3 Preheat the oven to 220°C/425°F/gas 7. Remove the gammon from its cooking stock, transfer to a small roasting tin and set aside. The cooking stock will be used to make the sauce, so check that it has not become too salty from the gammon (if it has, add a little more water to dilute the salt). Boil, uncovered, over a high heat until it has reduced to about 500ml (17fl oz); this could take about 10 minutes of boiling.

4 Strain the liquid through a sieve into a clean pan, rubbing any pieces of apple through the sieve too so that the flesh is in the sauce; leave behind only the skins. Taste the sauce and adjust seasoning to taste. If you want it sweeter, add the demerara sugar; you almost certainly won't need any salt.

5 Cut the rind from the gammon, leaving a thin layer of fat, and discard the rind. With a small sharp knife, score the fat into diamonds. Make a glaze by spooning about 4 tablespoons of the sauce over the gammon and then sprinkling with the sugar and chilli powder. Pour a splash of boiling water into the tin to stop the juices burning, and roast in the preheated oven for 15 minutes, until browned and caramelised. Keep warm while you finish the sauce.

SERVES 6

1.2kg (2lb 10oz) boneless gammon joint (we used unsmoked but smoked would work too)
500ml (17fl oz) cider
1 litre (1¾ pints) cloudy apple juice
2 sharp green apples, cored and cut into rough chunks
2 x 8cm (3¼in) pieces cinnamon stick
3-4 fresh red chillies, seeds removed, cut into quarters
1 tbsp coarsely crushed coriander seeds

FOR THE SAUCE

1 tbsp demerara sugar, or to taste
1 heaped tbsp cornflour

FOR THE GLAZE

4 tbsp sauce (above)
1 tbsp demerara sugar
¼ tsp chilli powder

Continues overleaf

6 Reheat the remaining strained sauce gently until it reaches a simmer. Blend the cornflour in a little cold water to a smooth paste, and stir about half of it into the sauce, stirring continuously. A creamy consistency is better than a very thick sauce, but if you prefer yours thicker, add a little more blended cornflour. To serve, place gammon slices on individual plates and pour over the sauce, and accompany with Spiced Red Cabbage (see page 186) and Green Chilli Mash (see page 187).

Originally created for using on meats for the barbecue, I discovered that this marinade also makes for a superb roasted joint of pork. You can, however, also use the marinade for its original purpose and soak diced loin of pork in it before placing it on the barbecue, or it will even work on pork chops, cooked under a grill.

Cyrus's
ROAST MARINATED PORK

1 Put all the marinade ingredients into a blender, and blitz to a fine paste. Rub the marinade all over the pork, cover and refrigerate for up to 8 hours or overnight.

2 Preheat the oven to 160°C/325°F/gas 3. Place the pork in a baking tin, cover with aluminium foil and cook for 2½ hours.

3 Increase the oven temperature to 180°C/350°F/gas 4 and remove the foil from the pork, and cook for a further 45 minutes. The meat should now be meltingly soft, and you should be able to pull it apart easily. Remove the joint, put it on a serving platter and cover loosely with foil while you make the gravy.

4 Put the onions into the tin in which the pork was cooked, and add the stock or water. Using a wooden spoon, scrape all the juicy, crusty bits from the bottom of the tin. Transfer the sauce to a saucepan and cook over a medium heat for around 10 minutes until the onions are soft and the sauce is the consistency you prefer. Season to taste and serve with the pork.

SERVES 6
1.5kg (3lb) rolled pork shoulder, skin scored, rind on

FOR THE MARINADE
100ml (3½fl oz) cider vinegar
30ml (1¼fl oz) lemon juice
10g (¼oz) dried red chillies
2–3 fresh green chillies, seeds removed if liked
4–6 black peppercorns
8–10 garlic cloves
5–7.5cm (2–3in) piece fresh root ginger, sliced
1 tsp cumin seeds
10g (¼oz) cassia bark
3–4 cloves
1 tsp sea salt

FOR THE GRAVY
2 onions, sliced
250–300ml (9fl oz–½ pint) vegetable stock or water

SPICE FOCUS
CASSIA BARK

I am very fond of cassia because its flavour was so much part of my childhood. It was one of the cheaper spices, so Mum used it a lot, particularly in meat dishes. Like most Parsee mums, she would cook us *kharu gos*, a traditional lamb dish. You start with a ginger and garlic masala or paste (as usual), then you add toasted spices – cassia, green and black cardamoms, cloves and dried red chillies.

That particular flavour of childhood lingers in your mouth, no matter how old you become, and I can still visualise my mother cooking it, see that old brass pot, Mum stirring with her tongs. She would then plonk it into the much-loved pressure cooker that she had received as a wedding gift on June 1, 1950. I have it at home: I've had to replace the rubber rings but it's still going strong! And I am still cooking Mum's *kharu gos*, although now I use a whole lamb and at least four pressure cookers!

Cassia, like cinnamon, comes from the aromatic bark of an evergreen tree native to India and northern Burma. It is now mostly grown in China, and is known as Chinese cassia or Chinese (or bastard) cinnamon (and used instead of true cinnamon in America). Cassia is harvested in much the same way as cinnamon, but it's tougher: often the bark is retained, and the quills are formed of only one layer rather than many layers as in cinnamon. The flavour is sweeter and more intense than cinnamon. It is also much harder to grind: if you need to grind it you will have to do it more than once, sieving each time.

Because it is so pungent, cassia is ideally suited to flavouring rich meat dishes, whether Indian or British. The Roast Marinated Pork on the previous page is especially delicious. As Tony said, if he were a Middle White porker, such as the delightful pigs we met while in Hastings (see page 136), that's how he'd like to finish up his life! And the flavour of cassia spices both our Coronation chicken (see page 97) and our recipe for shepherd's pie (see page 149). It is a cornerstone of the Parsee classic, lamb dhansak, and is even used in the pulao that traditionally accompanies it. One of the Chinese five spices, cassia is also good with many vegetables, and with some fruits, whether it's used whole or ground.

You can occasionally find cassia buds, which are very like cloves; these are less pungent than the bark. The leaves of a related tree are also aromatic, known as *tej-pat*, which are used in the same way as bay leaves. Cassia is used in treatments for minor ailments in India (coughs, colds and the like), and its leaves can apparently be used as a very effective mosquito repellent!

In Goa, once an overseas province of Portugal, there are many dishes influenced by Portuguese originals. The Goan version of pulled pork – so named because the meat is so tender when cooked that you can literally pull it apart – is a meal for times of celebration, and this version makes an interesting alternative to a traditional Sunday roast. Serve it in lettuce cups with the coleslaw on page 191.

Cyrus's

PULLED PORK WITH CINNAMON & CLOVE

1 First make the masala marinade. With a pestle and mortar, coarsely crush together the cassia bark or cinnamon and cloves. Gently toast this mixture in a dry frying pan over a low heat until a spicy fragrance emanates from the pan. Tear the red chillies into pieces and add to the pan. Continue to dry-fry the mixture for a short while but do not burn. Set aside to cool.

2 Put the cooled spice mix in a blender. Add all of the remaining masala ingredients and blend the mixture to a relatively fine paste. Taste and adjust seasoning if you like.

3 Rub the masala all over the pork, and place the meat in a dish in which it fits snugly. Set aside any remaining masala. Cover the meat and set aside in the refrigerator, if possible for a few hours.

4 Preheat the oven to 180°C/350°F/gas 4. Pour the oil into a roasting tin and heat on the hob over a medium heat. Scrape any excess masala from the marinated pork, place the pork in the roasting tin and brown well on all sides. Transfer to the oven and cook for 30 minutes.

5 Reduce the oven heat to minimum. (You can now pour a few tablespoons of marinade over the pork for extra flavour. Any leftover marinade can be set aside to use for another dish.) Cover the pork tightly with aluminium foil, well tucked in so that the pork steams in the tin and the meat literally falls off when cooked. Cook for a further 3–3½ hours if using a rolled joint; if using smaller pieces or individual chops, adjust your cooking time accordingly. Meanwhile, you can make the coleslaw (see page 191) if using.

6 Remove the pork from the oven and shred using two forks.

7 To serve, put some pork on top of a lettuce leaf. Top with some coleslaw (if using) or some coriander.

SERVES 6–8

2kg (4lb 8oz) rolled pork loin
    or shoulder or collar
50ml (2fl oz) vegetable or
    rapeseed oil
baby gem lettuce leaves, cleaned
    and well drained, to serve
3 tbsp fresh coriander, to garnish

FOR THE MASALA MARINADE

1 tbsp broken pieces cassia
    bark or cinnamon
15 cloves
2 large dried red chillies
5cm (2in) piece fresh root ginger,
    roughly chopped
4 garlic cloves
2 small red onions, coarsely cut
1 longish fresh green chilli
½ heaped tsp turmeric
2½ tbsp tamarind paste
100ml (3½fl oz) palm vinegar
    (if not available use cider
    vinegar)
½ tbsp brown sugar
25ml (1fl oz) sunflower or
    rapeseed oil
½ tbsp salt

This was born out of my hatred of wasting food – we had some leftover dhal, so rather than throw it away I decided to spice it up and use it as a stuffing for some pork. It's a real crowd-pleaser, and so easy to do once you've tried it. If you want to mix things up, try this with the Wild West Beans on page 66 instead of the dhal.

Tony's
LOIN OF PORK WITH DHAL STUFFING

1 To make the dhal stuffing, put the washed lentils in a pan, pour in enough cold water to cover the lentils by 2cm (¾in) and bring to the boil. Use a slotted spoon to skim off any froth that rises to the surface. Add all of the remaining dhal stuffing ingredients except the oil, cumin seeds and asafoetida, and cook over a medium heat for about 15 minutes until the lentils are tender. Most of the water should have evaporated.

2 Heat the oil in a small frying pan and then add the cumin seeds. When they start to pop (this should take place in less than 30 seconds) add the asafoetida, then pour everything including the oil onto the dhal. Season with a good pinch of salt, and tip the dhal onto a dish or tray to cool while you preheat the oven to 220°C/425°F/gas 7 and prepare the meat.

3 Put the pork skin-side down on a work surface and lightly score the meat with a sharp knife. Rub the garlic all over the meat, season well with salt and pepper and sprinkle over the lemon zest. Spread the cooled dhal over the meat, leaving a gap of a couple of centimetres along each edge. Carefully roll up the pork loin tightly, ensuring the dhal stuffing remains inside. Use butcher's string to make ties at 2cm (¾in) intervals.

4 Oil a roasting tin, then put the joint on it and sprinkle it with a little salt. Roast in the preheated oven for 20 minutes, then reduce the oven to 190°C/375°F/gas 5 and roast for a further 45 minutes per kg (2lb 4oz), which for this amount of meat will be just under 2 hours.

5 Remove the pork from the oven, cover tightly with aluminium foil and leave to rest for at least 15 minutes. To crisp the crackling further, heat some olive oil in a pan and roll the joint in it until it spits and blisters. Serve with apple sauce flavoured with clove.

SERVES 12
2.5kg (5lb 8oz) pork loin, butterflied (you can ask the butcher to do this)
3 garlic cloves, crushed
zest of 1 lemon
1 tbsp rapeseed oil or vegetable oil
sea salt and freshly ground black pepper

FOR THE DHAL STUFFING
150g (5oz) split red lentils, rinsed well under cold running water
75g (3oz) tinned tomatoes, chopped
1 onion, finely chopped
1 tsp crushed garlic
1 tsp crushed fresh root ginger
1 tsp garam masala
½ tsp chilli powder
½ tsp turmeric
1 tbsp rapeseed oil or vegetable oil
½ tsp cumin seeds
a pinch of asafoetida

There's nothing better than a juicy, crispy, lush Scotch pie – unless of course you add spices to it. The sweet, fatty taste of the lamb mince is paired with white pepper, nutmeg, coriander, cumin and some chilli. It's fantastic for picnics or lunches. Ideally, you need to make this a day in advance to give the pie time to set. If you have time, refrigerate the cooled pie for at least 2 hours before trying to remove it from the tin.

Tony

MCSĪNGH'S SCOTCH PĪE

1 Heat a large frying pan and toast the cumin seeds for a few minutes, then set aside. Heat the oil in the same pan and fry the onion, garlic, chilli, pepper and a good pinch of salt for around 8 minutes, until there is no moisture left. Remove from the heat, stir in the toasted cumin seeds, ground mace (or nutmeg) and ground coriander. Leave to cool.

2 In a large bowl mix the minced lamb, pepper, fresh coriander, and the cool spiced onion mixture until combined. Preheat the oven to 200°C/400°F/gas 6, and generously grease a 20cm (8in) loose-bottomed round cake tin with lard.

3 To make the pastry, sift the flour and salt in a large bowl and make a well in the centre. Put the water, milk and lard in a saucepan and heat gently. When the lard has melted, increase the heat and bring to the boil. Pour the boiling liquid into the flour, and use a wooden spoon to combine until cool enough to handle. Bring together into a ball.

4 Dust a work surface with flour and, working quickly, knead the dough briefly – it will be soft and moist. Set aside a third of the pastry and roll the rest out on a well-floured surface. Line the pie dish with the pastry, pressing it right up the sides until it pokes just over the top of the tin.

5 Add the filling into the pastry-lined tin bit by bit. As you reach the top, form a slight peak. Roll out the remaining pastry and top the pie with it. Pinch the edges to seal and trim the excess. Poke a hole in the top of the pie and insert a small tube made from aluminium foil to allow steam to escape. Brush with egg yolk, and bake on a shelf in the oven for 30 minutes (put a tray on the shelf below to catch any drips). Reduce the temperature to 160°C/325°F/gas 3 and cook for a further 1¼ hours until golden brown. Leave to cool completely.

6 Run a knife around the edge of the pie, remove from the tin and serve.

SERVES 6–8

2 tsp cumin seeds
1 tbsp rapeseed oil or vegetable oil, plus extra for greasing
2 medium red onions, finely chopped
6 garlic cloves, crushed
3 green chillies, seeds removed if liked, finely chopped
1 large red pepper, seeds removed, finely chopped
1 tsp ground mace or grated nutmeg
2 tsp ground coriander
1kg (2lb 4oz) lamb mince
1 tsp freshly ground white pepper
3 tbsp chopped fresh coriander
salt

FOR THE HOT WATER PASTRY

340g (12oz) plain flour, plus extra for flouring
½ tsp salt
90ml (3fl oz) water
90ml (3fl oz) milk
150g (5oz) lard, chopped into cubes, plus extra for greasing
1 egg yolk, beaten, for brushing

Cyrus's
PIG
FARMING
HASTINGS

I believe the Portuguese stayed on in India because of pork. They chose Goa, one of the most pork-friendly states, rather than Kerala. (And they could convert the Hindus of Goa; the Muslims of Kerala were another matter.) There are still many Goan pork specialities, which are Portuguese in origin. The most famous is vindaloo – from the Portuguese *vindalho*, wine vinegar and garlic – which has changed somewhat from its milder origins!

In India pork production is a secondary business: pigs are allowed to look after themselves, to forage on anything and everything they can find. This exposes them to infection, and so as soon as a piece of local pork is bought, Indian women will apply salt and turmeric: the salt to withdraw bacteria, the turmeric to suffocate the bacteria. The pork is then cooked slowly, for a long time, to make it as safe as possible.

So British pork has been a revelation to me, and I think it is the best in the world. I cook it much as I might in India, but the flavour is wonderful, and there is so much tasty fat – for crackling – and marbling through the meat. Try my Roast Marinated Pork (see page 126), pulled pork (see page 130) and cider-soaked gammon (see page 123), Tony's stuffed loin of pork (see page 133), and his to-die-for ribs (see page 120). They're

all so good because pork can take the most pungent of spices, among them cassia, star anise, cloves, chillies and pepper. It's one of my absolute favourite meats.

I am also very partial to the pig itself. They say that a dog looks up to you, a cat looks down at you, but a pig looks you straight in the eye. I used to breed pigs when I worked in Goa, some 300 of them, and it's true, they're very intelligent animals, always thinking about something.

So, pig-lover that I am, I was pleased to be able to introduce Tony to a couple who breed Middle White pigs on their smallholding in East Sussex. Roland and Jane Horton both work elsewhere, but devote their spare time to producing a variety of rare breeds. Roland says there are less than 400 breeding Middle White sows in the world, and it's up to enthusiasts like him to keep the breed going. (It's really not all that dissimilar to wildlife charities fighting to protect the 450 or so Siberian tigers left.)

Middle Whites, known as the 'London Porker', are so rare now because, post World War Two, the British government criticised farmers for producing pigs that were too small, with too much fat. This, among other factors, caused breeders to change their habits and many native breeds fell out of popular use – for instance, the pig that I usually favour, the British Lop, is even more threatened than the Middle White. We need loads of people who are willing to pay just that little bit more for good pork: the greater the demand for the meat of these delicious rare-breed animals, the better the chance they have of survival.

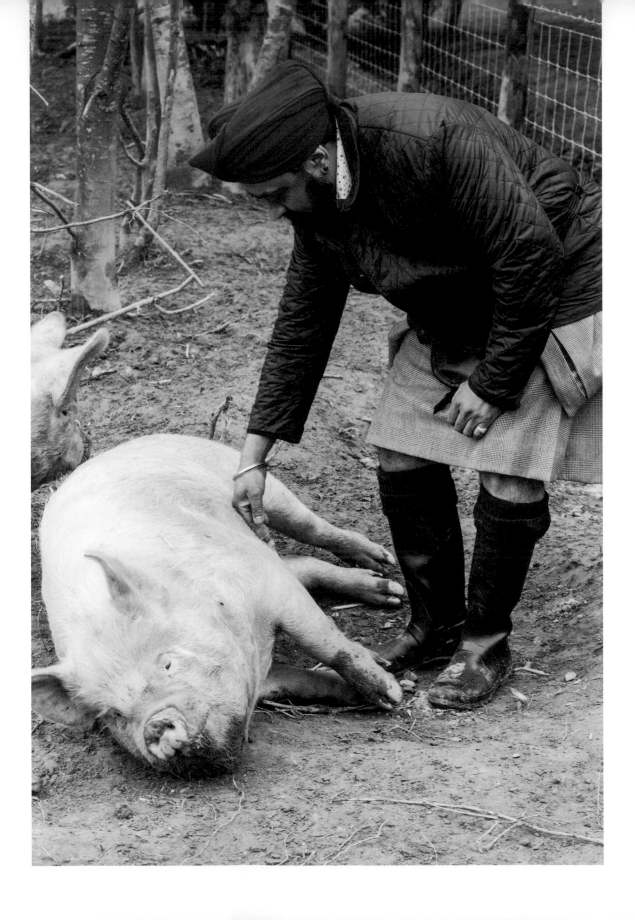

I used to make this to use up marrows from my old next-door neighbour's allotment. God love her, she'd keep bringing round such huge marrows for us to eat I wouldn't know what to do with them! It works really well with courgettes too, and is a great way to get kids to eat their greens – my kids love it. But put in plenty of bacon and fennel, it goes without saying.

Tony's

BACON & SPICY COURGETTE

1 If using marrow, cut it lengthways; scoop out the seeds with a spoon and discard. Cut the courgette or marrow into ½cm (¼in) slices. Lay these on a tray or large dish, scatter lightly with salt and leave for an hour. Rinse in cold water, drain in a colander and pat dry.

2 Drain the marrow or courgette in a colander and pat dry with kitchen paper, then season with pepper. Heat the oil in a large frying pan, then over a high heat and working in batches to avoid overcrowding the pan, sauté the courgette or marrow for 3–4 minutes, turning the slices over every so often until lightly coloured and tender.

3 In a heavy-bottomed pan, melt the butter and add the onion, garlic, bacon, fennel and cumin, and cook gently for 3–4 minutes until the onion is soft and the bacon is cooked. Remove from the heat and stir in the breadcrumbs, parsley and tarragon, and season with salt and pepper to taste.

4 Preheat the grill to medium. Transfer the courgette or marrow to a heatproof serving dish. Scatter the breadcrumb mixture over the top and grill until lightly browned. Serve immediately.

SERVES 4 AS A STARTER OR ACCOMPANIMENT TO MEAT OR FISH

500g (1lb 2oz) courgette or young marrow
1–2 tbsp rapeseed oil
30g (1¼oz) lightly salted butter
1 large onion, finely chopped
6 small garlic cloves, crushed
6 rashers of streaky bacon, finely chopped
1 tsp fennel seeds, toasted in a dry frying pan and ground
1 tsp cumin seeds
30g (1¼oz) fresh white breadcrumbs (approx 1 slice of bread)
1 tbsp chopped fresh parsley
1 tbsp chopped fresh tarragon
salt and freshly ground black pepper

This is simple, easy to prepare and will add some fun to a Sunday lunch or special occasion. In India, generally the entire rack of lamb is bought and then prepared at home – with the trimmed meat being used to make a delicious gravy. But, having said that, it's much easier to come home with a pre-trimmed rack of lamb!

Cyrus's

CUTLETS OF LAMB, PARSEE-STYLE

1 Sprinkle the cutlets with a little salt and set aside while you make the marinade.

2 To make the marinade, put the ginger and garlic into a mini food-processor and blend to a paste with 2–3 tbsp water or as needed; alternatively, blend the ginger and garlic with a pestle and mortar, or finely grate the ginger and crush the garlic by hand, then add the water. Add all of the remaining marinade ingredients and mix well. Rub the mixture all over the cutlets, then cover and refrigerate for 4–6 hours.

3 Preheat the oven to 200°C/400°F/gas 6. Arrange the cutlets in a single layer, with a gap between each one, on a rack suspended over an oven tray, or in one or two oven trays depending on size. Cook on the top shelf of the oven for 6–8 minutes (a few minutes longer if the cutlets are particularly thick), turning halfway through cooking. If you are cooking the meat in two trays, you may need to swap the trays over halfway through. The lamb should still be a little pink and juicy in the middle. Serve immediately.

NOTE: Prepare whatever you are to serve with the cutlets – such as roast potatoes, gravy, rice or salad – before you cook the meat. When the meat is cooked, the pan drippings can be saved for the next day, to make a gravy for example, or to add a great flavour to some mince.

SERVES 4-6
18 lamb cutlets, French trimmed (can be cut from a French-trimmed rack of lamb)
salt

FOR THE MARINADE
8cm (3¼in) piece fresh root ginger, roughly chopped
4 garlic cloves
1 tsp ground cumin
2 tsp ground coriander
½ tsp ground turmeric
1 tsp red chilli powder
2 tbsp vegetable oil or rapeseed oil

Mince of all types, when cooked with the right balance of spices and condiments, gives a meal full of beautiful flavours and aromas, and can be served in any number of ways. Here we bring you a simple lamb mince which can be served either on its own with some Indian breads, or for a slight twist try it with a fried egg on top, or scrambled with egg.

Cyrus's

NICELY SPICY LAMB KHEEMA

1 To make the ginger-garlic-chilli paste, heat a small frying pan over medium heat and dry-fry the cumin and coriander seeds for about 1 minute until toasted. Grind in a spice grinder or with a pestle and mortar. Tip into a mini food-processor or blender with the remaining paste ingredients and 1–2 tbsp water, and blend to a paste.

2 In a heavy-bottomed pan or casserole dish heat the oil over a medium heat and fry the cassia or cinnamon, cardamom and cloves for 1–2 minutes until fragrant. Add the chopped onion and fry for 10 minutes until softened and browned.

3 Add the chilli powder, turmeric and ginger-garlic-chilli paste, and cook for 3–4 minutes until the mix is golden and fragrant (add a splash of water if it starts to stick to the pan). Add the tomato purée and cook for 1 minute, then add the lamb mince, stir well to break up any lumps and cook for 5 minutes, stirring often. Add a splash of water if the mix starts to stick to the pan.

4 Add the tomatoes, dried red chillies if using, and the boiling water. Stir to mix and simmer for 20 minutes until the liquid is reduced to a rich sauce. Season to taste and stir in the chopped coriander and mint. Serve with rotis.

SERVES 3–4

FOR THE GINGER-GARLIC-CHILLI PASTE
1 tsp cumin seeds
1 tbsp coriander seeds
5cm (2in) piece fresh root ginger, sliced
5 garlic cloves, chopped
2 fresh green chillies, seeds removed if liked, roughly chopped

FOR THE KHEEMA
2–3 tbsp vegetable oil or rapeseed oil
7cm (3in) piece cassia bark or cinnamon stick
4 cardamom pods, bruised with a rolling pin to crack open
4 cloves
2 onions, finely chopped
1 tsp red chilli powder
½ tsp turmeric
2 tbsp tomato purée
500g (1lb 2oz) lean lamb mince
3 tomatoes, chopped
2 dried red chillies (optional)
250ml (9fl oz) boiling water
3 tbsp chopped fresh coriander
1 heaped tbsp chopped fresh mint
salt

SPICE
FOCUS
CLOVES

The evergreen clove tree originated in the Moluccas, the famed 'Spice Islands', now part of Indonesia. What I think of as the 'king of spices' is the unopened, long flower buds that appear twice a year. When these turn pink, just before they open into flowers, they are picked from the tree and dried. Although Indonesia produces a vast clove crop still, it is mostly for internal consumption, and today Zanzibar, Madagascar and Tanzania dominate the world trade.

The flavour of cloves is warm, with hints of pepper, and a sharpness from its eugenol content: it is assertive, so cloves should be used fairly sparingly. A couple of cloves stuck in an onion for a bread sauce, or a béchamel or cheese sauce (as for cauliflower) are quite enough. Cloves lend a warm depth of flavour to many meat dishes, particularly pork dishes such as the Goan sorpotel, or my Roast Marinated Pork (see page 126) – and I use at least ten cloves in my lamb stew on page 150!

A classic roast ham is usually studded with cloves for flavour, but given that most of the flavour is absorbed by the fat, I think this is rather a waste of cloves! Cloves are an essential constituent of garam masalas, of Chinese five-spice powder (along with star anise, cassia, fennel seeds and Sichuan peppercorns), and of the French *quatre épices* (along with dried ginger, black pepper and nutmeg). The flavour goes well with fruit too – classically with apples in a pie or compote (or indeed a sauce for pork) – as well as many vegetables like pumpkin. I love them in rice dishes too. Use cloves whole in mulled wines, cider, ales and teas, and in a digestive *paan*. I find that the warm smells and flavours brought by cooking with cloves always sends out a greeting: 'welcome to my house'.

Cloves have also been valued medicinally over the centuries. They contain eugenol, which is strongly antiseptic, so were used in pomanders in the Middle Ages to ward off the plague; our oranges of today, studded with cloves, keep moths, rather than pestilence, at bay! The Chinese used cloves to cure hiccups and impotence, and in Ayurvedic medicine, a clove tea was thought to be good for fatigue and for coughs and catarrh. Cloves can slightly numb your tongue when sucked, so historically they have been used for dental problems, and clove oil is actually used in many toothpastes.

Buy cloves whole if you can, as they will contain the most flavour. Keep for up to a year in an airtight jar. It is hard to grind cloves at home, and an electric grinder must be used. Bought ground cloves actually last quite a long time, primarily because the spice contains so much essential oil. Keep that under airtight conditions for up to four months.

Minced lamb is very popular in India, not just because it tastes great but also because it is an ideal way to stretch a small quantity into a large family dish. This is a simple take on a favourite of mine – the Country Captain, or Indian shepherd's pie, which featured among the dishes that I cooked for Her Majesty The Queen on her Diamond Jubilee tour.

Cyrus's

SHEPHERD'S PIE WITH OOMPH AND AAH

1 First prepare the topping. If you're in a hurry, cut the potatoes into chunks, boil them in salted water for 20 minutes, then drain and mash. But for the best results, bake the potatoes: preheat the oven to 200°C/400°F/gas 6, place the potatoes directly on the oven shelf and bake for about 1 hour. Remove the baked potatoes from the oven, and while they are still warm cut them in half and scoop the flesh into a bowl. Push the flesh through a fine sieve or a potato ricer into another bowl.

2 Whichever method you use to cook the potatoes, once they are mashed mix in the eggs (you can use just the yolks if you prefer, and save the whites for another purpose), along with some cream to loosen the mix. Season with a pinch or two of ground nutmeg, some finely chopped green chilli, crushed cumin seeds and salt and pepper, and mix thoroughly.

3 Now prepare the filling. Heat a large casserole dish, add the oil, and when it's hot add the bay leaves and cassia or cinnamon, then fry on a medium heat for a couple of minutes. Turn the heat off, add the butter and let it melt.

4 Put all of the remaining filling ingredients except the fresh coriander in a large bowl and mix thoroughly. Turn a medium heat back on underneath the casserole dish and add the filling mixture, along with 100ml (3½fl oz) water. Stir and cook for 5–6 minutes. Stir once more and cook for a further 10–15 minutes, then remove the lid and cook until the mixture is nearly dry. Meanwhile, preheat the oven to 200°C/400°F/gas 6.

5 Stir the chopped coriander into the cooked mixture and pour into a baking dish. Discard the bay leaves and cassia or cinnamon and level the surface. Cover the mince with the spiced mash topping and cook on the top shelf of the oven for 15–20 minutes until nicely browned. Serve with some crusty bread.

SERVES 4–6

FOR THE TOPPING

4–5 large baking potatoes
3 eggs
25ml (1fl oz) double or single cream
pinch of ground nutmeg
1–2 green bird's-eye chillies, seeds removed if liked, finely chopped
½ tsp cumin seeds, lightly toasted in a dry frying pan and crushed with a pestle and mortar
salt and freshly ground black pepper

FOR THE FILLING

1 tbsp vegetable oil or rapeseed oil
4 bay leaves
8cm (3¼in) piece cassia bark or cinnamon stick
15g (½oz) butter
500g (1lb 2oz) lamb mince
2–3 onions, finely chopped
5 garlic cloves, crushed
1 tbsp freshly grated root ginger
1 tsp turmeric
2 tbsp ground coriander
1 tbsp ground cumin
1 tsp garam masala
2 heaped tbsp tomato purée
2 heaped tbsp chopped fresh coriander
salt

This subtle, mellow stew is often cooked in Indian people's homes and is great for the whole family. It shows how simple dishes of European origin have been adapted and adopted into the cuisine of the subcontinent. As an alternative to lamb, I urge you to try mutton – ask your butcher to source meat approved by the Mutton Renaissance Club. The dish can be easily cooked in a pressure cooker or in the oven, while you get on with life – adjust the timings accordingly.

Cyrus's

LAMB STEW WITH BLACK PEPPER, COCONUT & CLOVE

1 Place the prepared lamb or mutton into a casserole dish that has a tight-fitting lid. Add the cinnamon, cloves and peppercorns, and enough cold water to just cover the meat. Cover the pan tightly (line the edge of the lid in aluminium foil to increase the tightness if necessary). Bring to the boil, then reduce the heat to low and simmer for 30 minutes.

2 Partly uncover the pan, allowing steam to escape and the liquid to reduce, and continue to simmer on the lowest heat for a further 1 hour.

3 Meanwhile, boil the cubed potatoes until soft, then drain and set aside. In a separate pan, heat the oil and cook the onions gently until soft, giving them a good seasoning of salt. Add the flour to the onions and stir for 3–4 minutes until the flour is absorbed into the oil and is cooked.

4 Add the onion mixture to the meat pan and mix well. Bring to the boil, then reduce the heat to low and simmer for 10–15 minutes, stirring, until well combined and thickened. Add the coconut milk and simmer for a further 30 minutes, stirring frequently. Check the texture of the lamb or mutton: it will go from being quite hard to very tender quite suddenly; this is the point at which the stew is ready.

5 When the meat is tender add the cooked potatoes, and simmer for a minute until the potatoes are warmed through. Taste and adjust the seasoning if necessary. Serve with crusty bread and some vegetables.

NOTE: As an extra touch, add parsley or coriander before serving. The boiled potatoes could be fried and served on top of the stew, perhaps sprinkled with chopped coriander, or some crisp fried curry leaves, which would go well with coconut and spices. You could also add a whole split fresh green chilli to the dish, but the flavour would veer away from the original.

SERVES 4–6

1kg (2lb 4oz) boneless lamb shoulder or mutton haunch, well cleaned of all skin, sinew, fat, gristle and cut into 1cm (½in) cubes

4 x 2.5cm (1in) pieces cinnamon stick, discard tiny pieces that break off

10–15 cloves

1 tsp black peppercorns, or more to taste

3 large potatoes, peeled, cut into large cubes and well rinsed

2 tbsp rapeseed oil or vegetable oil

2 red onions, cut into quarters and sliced

1½ tbsp plain flour

1 x 400ml (14fl oz) tin coconut milk

salt

This is an absolute cracker from my mum. She was a great, adventurous cook, and we loved a good lamb spag bol when I was smaller. But my grandad wasn't quite so adventurous and wouldn't eat British or European food when he came to visit, so my mum would rustle up meatball masala to keep everybody happy. Lovely lamb meatballs in a rich masala sauce – us kids loved it, and so did my grandad.

Tony's

MEATBALL MASALA

1 Heat a small pan and fry the fennel seeds for a minute or so, until lightly toasted. Remove and grind in a pestle and mortar. Finely chop the red onions and chillies, and grate the garlic cloves and ginger.

2 Heat the oil in a pan over a medium heat, then sauté the onions with a pinch of salt until soft. Add the garlic, ginger and chillies, and cook for a further 5 minutes. Add the garam masala and ground fennel seeds and mix well until mixed through. Set aside to cool.

3 To make the spice paste, mix together all of the ingredients with 2 tablespoons of water. Set aside.

4 When the spiced onion mixture has cooled, transfer it to a large bowl. Add the minced lamb and chopped coriander, and mix well. Form the mixture into golf-ball-sized balls (it should make some 24 meatballs). Refrigerate for at least 30 minutes.

5 To make the sauce, heat the oil in a large pan over medium heat. Break the cinnamon stick into 2 pieces and add it to the pan with the onion and a pinch of salt. Fry until the onions are soft. Add the garlic and stir-fry for 2 minutes, then add the ginger and cook for a further minute.

6 Add the spice paste to the pan, reduce the heat and stir-fry for about 2 minutes. Add the tinned tomatoes, stir and cook for further 2–3 minutes. Add the potatoes and cook for about 2 minutes.

7 Add the meatballs and enough warm water to cover the potatoes and meatballs. Simmer for about 25 minutes until the potatoes are tender and meat is cooked through.

8 Add the peas and green chillies and season with salt to taste; cook for a minute or two. Serve with natural yoghurt and your favourite Indian bread.

SERVES 4

1 tsp fennel seeds
2 small red onions
3 fresh green chillies
10 small garlic cloves
7.5cm (3in) fresh root ginger
2 tbsp vegetable oil or rapeseed oil
2 tsp garam masala
700g (1½lb) minced lamb
30g (1¼oz) fresh coriander, very finely chopped
salt

FOR THE SPICE PASTE

2 tsp ground coriander
1 tsp ground cumin
1 tsp turmeric
½ tsp chilli powder
1 tsp garam masala

FOR THE SAUCE

2 tbsp rapeseed oil or vegetable oil
5cm (2in) stick cinnamon
1 red onion, finely chopped
4 garlic cloves, crushed
3.5cm (1½in) fresh root ginger, grated
1 x 400g (14oz) tin chopped tomatoes
200g (7oz) waxy potatoes, peeled and diced into 2cm (¾in) cubes
100g (4oz) frozen peas
2–3 green chillies, finely chopped
salt

One of the many great representatives of Indian cuisine is the venerable *sheek kavaab* (kebab), a street-food speciality. This simple and delicious recipe is based on the kebabs my father often put together after his hunting trips, using venison mince. Here I use beef, but the recipe adapts well to other meats, such as lamb, chicken and turkey, though the meat should always be lean.

Cyrus

DAD'S BEEF KEBABS

1 Place all of the ingredients except the oil or water for shaping in a large bowl, and mix by hand really thoroughly, ensuring all the ingredients are combined. To check the seasoning, fry a small amount of the mixture until cooked through, taste and adjust the seasoning if needed. Cover the uncooked mince mixture and refrigerate for 6–8 hours. Meanwhile, ensure the skewers fit inside your griddle pan; square skewers are best, thin round ones may not hold the weight of the mince.

2 Take a ball of mince mixture about 5cm (2in) in diameter in one hand and a skewer in the other. Make the meatball as smooth as possible by tossing it like a ball in your hand. Positioning the ball at roughly the middle of the skewer, press around it so that the mince covers all around that part of the skewer.

3 Now apply a little oil or water to the palm that you use for the mince, and gently press the meat in the form of a sausage on the skewer. This takes a bit of practice, and you may find that the mince tends to fall off the skewer as you work. The trick is to form a ring between your forefinger and thumb, and use your other fingers to guide the mince; apply a gentle pressure, and push the mince upwards so that the 'sausage' thins itself out over the skewer. Ideally the size of the sausage should be around 2.5cm (1in) or a bit less in diameter.

4 Heat a griddle pan while you continue to form the mince into sausages on the skewers, until you have 8 skewers.

5 Cook in the hot griddle pan for approximately 8–10 minutes, rotating the kebabs as they cook. Take care not to overcook them as this makes them dry and chewy. They should ideally feel spongy but still nice and moist. Serve with fresh green chutney and an onion-based salad, and perhaps rolled into a chapatti or a flour tortilla to make a wrap.

SERVES 4

500g (1lb 2oz) minced beef
1 heaped tbsp finely chopped fresh coriander, including stalks
1 heaped tbsp finely chopped fresh mint leaves
2.5cm (1in) fresh root ginger, grated
2 garlic cloves, grated
2 fresh green chillies, seeds removed if liked, chopped
1 tsp lime juice
1 tsp garam masala
1 tsp ground cumin
1 heaped tsp ground coriander
1 tsp red chilli powder
½ tsp turmeric powder
1 tsp sunflower oil, rapeseed oil or water, for shaping
salt

8 skewers, square if available, to fit in griddle pan, soaked in water for 10 minutes if wooden

Cyrus's
CATTLE FARMING
SUFFOLK

For me, British beef is probably the best in the world. For a start it's quite cold in the UK, so animals bred outside develop a good covering of fat, which keeps the meat juicy. It also rains a lot here, which means beef grazing fields are green and superbly lush, which of course makes for wonderful meat.

To celebrate beef while filming the television series, we met Nick Thompson and Denise Thomas, who rear prize-winning Suffolk Red Polls, one of the oldest breeds in the country. The Red Poll is an all-round cow, giving both creamy milk and good meat. As you are unlikely to find this meat in your local supermarket, try to buy Aberdeen Angus or similar. Get your butcher to advise you, pointing you in the direction of aged, well-hung, well marbled meat.

I have always been fond of animals, particularly cows. Nick and Denise introduced me to the farm's prize cow, Rhiannon, who looked as if she were straight out of a Gainsborough painting. She was so graceful, so patient as I brushed her down. She was due to enter a competition the next day, which she duly won. What a cow!

I always have a lot of fun spicing up beef recipes. One of my favourites is very redolent of home: a version of a Persian-style kebab that my father used to make with venison (see page 154).

Chilli is predominant, but given a zing from fresh coriander and mint. Another mince recipe is a gourmet version of the American hamburger (see page 160). Here I used a Thai chilli for sharp heat, and crushed black peppercorns along with cumin, coriander, garlic and ginger. Peppercorns appear again in my tikka (see page 165), this time using good sirloin or fillet, cut into cubes, and marinated in a medley of ground spices before grilling. Wonderful served with cooling salads, and some rice.

Beef is not widely eaten in India, mainly because of the reverence that Hindus have for cows. Zoroastrians like myself revere cattle too, for one of them saved the infant Zarathustra from death during a stampede. Orthodox Sikhs do not eat meat at all, and all Sikhs have the same respect for the cow as their Hindu neighbours. Despite the theological debate surrounding the eating of meat, however, both Tony and I are keen carnivores.

What you will find in India is bull or buffalo meat. Both are beasts of burden, and the latter are used for milk as well; only when both are past their prime are they killed for meat. And as they won't have had wonderful grass to eat, they will be good and tough, and require long slow cooking, with lots of spices. Beef has the potential to carry quite powerful spicing, such as cassia, star anise, cloves, which are used in many beef curries.

Indians love minced meat, *kheema*, which is usually lamb, though beef is eaten by some. They make it into sturdily spiced kebabs, into little pies like samosas, into burgers, meatballs, and even eat it for breakfast. A ring of spiced mince is served with a coddled egg in the middle; you mix the egg into the mince, thus the name *keema ghotala*, 'confused mince'!

A wonderful burger, this is simple to put together, and shows what can result from thinking just a little bit differently. So, to bring out the best of your beef, choose the best-quality lean meat you can, be brave and have fun experimenting with combinations of ingredients – a little turmeric, for example, can really liven things up. For a truly exciting experience, serve it alongside some potato wedges with our spicy salt sprinkling.

Cyrus's

SPLENDIDLY SPICY BEEF BURGER

1 Heat the oil in a frying pan and cook the onions on a medium heat, stirring frequently, until soft and slightly coloured. The small amount of oil used in this recipe means the onions might stick to the pan at some point; if necessary, deglaze with a splash of water.

2 Add the ginger, garlic and green chilli and continue to fry until cooked and any liquid has evaporated. Transfer the mixture to a plate, spread out and allow to cool.

3 Preheat the oven to 200°C/400°F/gas 6. Bring a large pan of salted water to the boil and add the potato wedges. Boil for 5–6 minutes, then drain. Place the parboiled potatoes on a baking tray, drizzle with the oil, then toss to coat. Put the tray in the oven and roast for 20–25 minutes until golden and crisp. Mix the ingredients for the spice blend together in a small bowl and set aside until you serve.

4 Put the minced beef in a mixing bowl, add the onion mixture and all of the remaining ingredients, and mix well. (Mixing makes the meat more malleable and smoother; the more you work it, it the smoother it gets.) Shape into four to six burgers.

5 Heat a griddle pan, hot plate, frying pan or barbecue to hot. Brush the burgers with a little oil and cook: 4 minutes each side for a medium finish for six burgers, a little longer if you have made four larger burgers. Rest the burgers for a few minutes while you sprinkle the cooked potato wedges with the spice blend. Serve the burgers in buns, with the wedges alongside and some ketchup for dipping.

MAKES 4 LARGE, OR 6 MEDIUM BURGERS

1 tbsp sunflower oil or
   rapeseed oil, plus extra
   for brushing
1 large onion, finely chopped
2cm (¾in) piece fresh root
   ginger, very finely chopped
   or ground to a paste
2 garlic cloves, very finely
   chopped or ground to a paste
1 green Thai chilli, seeds
   removed, very finely chopped
800g (1lb 14oz) lean minced beef
2 tsp ground cumin
3 tsp ground coriander
1 tbsp tomato paste or purée
2 tbsp chopped fresh coriander
½ tsp garam masala
1–2 tsp salt
1 tsp black peppercorns, crushed

FOR THE SPICY POTATO WEDGES

1kg (2lb 4oz) potatoes, unpeeled,
   cut into wedges
1 tbsp rapeseed oil or
   vegetable oil
2 tsp ground cumin
2 tsp red chilli powder
1 tsp freshly ground white pepper
2 tsp salt
1 heaped tsp mango powder
   (optional)

This is a wonderful way of using steak. Ever since we introduced this at our restaurant it has been one of the most popular tikkas on the menu. We use British beef, which is normally of exceptional quality – I urge you to do the same. Consult your local butcher and enquire about the quality and maturity of your meat – they will be delighted that you've asked. For this recipe, marination should be carried out patiently, and overnight is best.

Cyrus's

BEEF TĪKKA WĪTH CRUSHED BLACK PEPPER

1 To make the marinade, heat a large frying pan over a low heat, then add the red chillies, peppercorns and the cumin and coriander seeds and dry-fry for 3–4 minutes, stirring often, until lightly toasted and aromatic. Cool and grind to a powder with a pestle and mortar or in a coffee grinder.

2 With a blender, purée the remaining marinade ingredients along with this spice powder, adding extra oil if needed to make a paste. Some tamarind pastes are very concentrated, so add this a little at a time until you find your preferred taste.

3 Place the beef cubes in a large bowl and add the marinade a little at a time, mixing well until the meat is thoroughly coated. You may not need all of the marinade, but be quite generous. Cover and leave to marinate in the fridge for at least 8 hours.

4 Preheat a barbecue or a griddle pan to hot. Cook the meat cubes (if using a griddle, don't overcrowd the pan) for 1 minute on each side, or until browned on the outside but still pink in the middle. Alternatively, push the beef cubes onto metal skewers, leaving a gap between each cube, and cook in the same manner.

SERVES 6

1.5kg (3lb) sirloin steak, trimmed and cut into 5cm (2in) cubes (or use well-hung beef fillet if it's a special occasion)

FOR THE MARINADE

4–8 hot dried red chillies, depending on how hot you want the marinade
1 tsp black peppercorns
1 heaped tsp cumin seeds
2 tbsp coriander seeds
6 garlic cloves
10cm (4in) piece fresh root ginger, roughly chopped
2 mild fresh green chillies, seeds removed if liked, and chopped
2 tsp red chilli powder
2 heaped tbsp tamarind paste
3–4 tbsp sunflower oil or rapeseed oil, or as needed to make a paste
salt

VEGETABLES, SIDES, SALADS & CHUTNEYS

7 Remove the pan from the heat. Add all of the remaining ingredients except the fresh coriander (and the bread), return to a low heat and cook gently until all the cheese has melted and the mixture starts to bubble at the edges – it will be very thick at this stage which is correct. Stir in the coriander, taste and adjust the seasoning if needed.

8 Heat the grill to maximum. Toast the bread, either under the grill on both sides or in a toaster. Dollop the rarebit mixture generously over the toast, place under the grill until bubbling and golden in places. Serve hot.

NOTES: Any leftover spice paste can be mixed with a little oil to make a delicious rub for chicken or meat.

Any leftover rarebit mix will keep well for 3–4 days in the fridge, stored in an airtight container which must be closed only when the mixture is totally cold. When cold it will apply like a firm spread but will still taste amazing. You can use it to stuff escalopes, chicken breast, croquettes and so on; when you cook you get the cheese oozing out.

25g (1oz) Cornish blue or other blue cheese, crumbled, or more to taste

3 egg yolks

2–3 tbsp English mustard

2–3 mild fresh green chillies, seeds removed, finely chopped

1 garlic clove, finely crushed (optional)

1 tsp crushed black peppercorns

1 heaped tbsp chopped fresh coriander

6–8 thick slices bread

pinch of salt

Cyrus's
SPICE FOCUS PEPPER

When I was a child, we bought our peppercorns from the local Philips Coffee and Tea shop, as pepper was grown amongst their coffee bushes. They would grind the peppercorns for you if you wanted, but we usually bought them whole. (Many pepper vendors would try to cheat by including dried papaya seeds.) Now, the British use pepper more than any other nation, and have it constantly on the dining table along with salt.

The most historically and economically important plant in the Piperaceae family is *Piper nigrum*, literally 'black pepper', once known as 'black gold'. The plant's seeds, the peppercorns, are the spice, and these grow on creeping vines native to the moist forests of India, Sri Lanka and Malaysia. The plants need shade, so are grown with other food plants.

Black, white and green peppercorns come from the same plant. Long flower spikes give way to dense spikes of seeds, which start off green and ripen to red. Green peppercorns are picked when green, then tinned or preserved in brine or oil. For black peppercorns, peppercorns just turning from green to red are dried in the sun until the outer husk turns black. White peppercorns are red or mature seeds which have been soaked and fermented in water: the outer husk is removed and then the inner seed is dried to the white peppercorn with which we are familiar.

Pepper gives a nice tingling on the tongue, and encourages saliva to be secreted, which is good for digestion. It gives flavour and warmth to food – at one point pepper, mustard and ginger provided the only heat in Indian cooking, before the arrival of the chilli pepper (no relation!). White pepper is perhaps slightly less aromatic than black, but the level of heat is much the same.

Pepper can be used whole, crushed or ground. Add peppercorns whole to stocks, soups and stews, to sausage and salami mixes. Crush them to coat a steak or chicken breast, when they add texture as well as flavour. Toast them before cracking, as you might cumin or coriander seeds, for added fragrance. Grind them into cake mixes, or spice mixtures such as the many marinades and meat rubs throughout the book. Cracked peppercorns are wonderful too, surprisingly, with fresh strawberries.

If you have a pepper grinder on the table while you eat, why not add some cumin or coriander to the grinder too, for a little extra flavour? Always grind pepper into or onto food just before eating, as its essential oils fade quickly. Never buy ready ground of either black or white – whole seeds are readily available and are vastly superior.

When I visited India for the first time, this was one of my favourite street foods. I first tasted it paired with a *really* spicy sauce – a green chilli, coriander, gingery sort of affair – but I like the simplicity of the pesto here. A must-try.

Tony's

KATĪ KEBAB & PARSLEY PESTO

1 Put all of the parsley pesto ingredients except the olive oil in a food-processor and blitz until finely chopped. Then pour the olive oil in slowly while continuing to blitz the mix to a thick paste. Season with salt to taste then set aside.

2 To make the kebabs, heat the oil in a frying pan over medium-high heat. Add the onion and fry for 2 minutes. Add the ginger and garlic and fry for 1 minute, then add the peppers and peas and fry for 3 minutes until just cooked but still crunchy.

3 Add the spices, the paneer or haloumi and a little salt (if you're using haloumi then leave the salt out – the cheese is salty enough already), and a splash of water if the spices are starting to stick to the pan, and fry for 2–3 minutes until the cheese is heated through (you can cover pan with a lid to speed things up).

4 To serve, warm the tortillas according to the packet instructions. Spread each with a good spoonful of pesto and then spoon the paneer filling down the middle of each tortilla. Roll up and serve straight away.

MAKES 4 KEBABS

FOR THE PARSLEY PESTO
50g (2oz) flat-leaf parsley leaves
25g (1oz) pine nuts
1 small garlic clove
20g (¾oz) Parmesan
75ml (2½fl oz) olive oil

FOR THE KEBAB
1½ tbsp vegetable or sunflower oil
1 small onion, thinly sliced
3cm (1¼in) piece fresh root ginger, finely chopped or grated
5 garlic cloves, well crushed
1 small red pepper, seeds removed, cut into 2cm- (¾in-) wide strips
50g (2oz) green peas (defrosted frozen peas are fine)
½ tsp chilli powder
½ tsp turmeric
200g (7oz) paneer or haloumi cheese, cut into rectangles about 2 x 5cm (¾ x 2in) and 1cm (½in) thick
salt
4 x 20cm (8in) tortilla breads, to serve

FRONT

This is a sort of savoury bread and butter pudding, made using the flavours of a korma sauce – cashew, almond, sultana, coconut. It's a nice way of introducing some delicate spice flavouring to a dish (I like serving it with a chicken breast), or is delicious on its own, perhaps served with a little salsa.

Tony's
KORMA PUDDING

1 Generously butter the insides of 6 x 175ml (6fl oz) dariole moulds or ramekins, then coat with the black sesame seeds, sprinkling out any excess.

2 Put the coconut in a pan, add the boullion powder, milk and cream, and stir well. Bring to the boil under a medium heat, then take the pan off the heat. Stir in the sultanas and both types of nut, and leave to cool to room temperature. Meanwhile, preheat the oven to 180°C/350°F/gas 4.

3 Put the kettle on to boil. Place the bread cubes in a large bowl. Stir the eggs into the cooled coconut and cream mixture, then pour this over the bread and mix. Mix in the chives and coriander, season with a pinch of salt and plenty of black pepper. Spoon into the prepared moulds.

4 Put the moulds in a roasting tin and carefully pour boiling water into the tin to come halfway up sides of the moulds. Bake for 15–20 minutes until golden and firm. Take the tin out of the oven and allow the puddings to rest, without removing them from the tin, then serve hot; alternatively, leave to cool completely and serve at room temperature.

MAKES 6 INDIVIDUAL PUDDINGS

softened butter, for greasing
50g (2oz) black sesame seeds, to coat
90g (3½oz) desiccated coconut
3 tsp boullion powder
225ml (8fl oz) milk
225ml (8fl oz) double cream
50g (2oz) sultanas (a mix of golden and regular if you have both)
45g (1¾oz) cashews, toasted in a dry frying pan and roughly chopped
45g (1¾oz) almonds, toasted in a dry frying pan and roughly chopped
½ loaf white bread, crusts removed, diced into 2cm (¾in) cubes (you want 150g/5oz prepared cubed bread)
3 eggs, lightly beaten
3 tbsp chopped fresh chives
3 tbsp chopped fresh coriander
salt and freshly ground black pepper

A simple, tasty salad to have on picnics on sunny days, or maybe by itself for a light lunch. It's really tasty with a few pieces of smoked salmon or some prawns on the side, if you want to make it a bit more substantial. I finely shred the ingredients to make a neater, prettier salad, but it's much quicker, and just as tasty, if you grate the mango instead.

Tony's

GREEN MANGO & CHĪLLĪ SALAD

1 Peel the mango and finely slice the flesh into a bowl. Discard the stone.

2 With a large pestle and mortar (or a mixing bowl and the end of a rolling pin), lightly bruise together the garlic, chilli and green beans. Add all of the remaining ingredients and bruise everything once again.

3 Add the shredded mango to the salad, mix well and serve.

SERVES 2–3 AS A SIDE DISH

1 green mango
2 garlic cloves, chopped
pinch of chopped red bird's-eye chilli
5 green beans, halved lengthways
2 tsp muscovado sugar
2 shallots, finely sliced
25g (1oz) roasted and salted peanuts, crushed
1 tbsp Thai fish sauce
½ tsp tamarind paste
8 cherry plum tomatoes, halved
juice of 1 lime

We were in Hastings and Cyrus was making some lovely spiced fish and chips (see page 62), so I thought, 'we've got to have some mushy peas to go with that!' Instead of using vinegar to bring a little sharpness, we've added some tamarind to give things a kick. It was delicious with the fish and chips, or it's great on its own, with a dollop of butter on top.

Tony's
MUSHY PEAS & TAMARIND

1 Wash the soaked peas under cold running water and place into a large saucepan.

2 Add water to cover, tip in the sugar and add salt and pepper to taste. Bring to the boil and skim off any froth that rises to the top of the pan with a spoon. Boil gently for about 30-40 minutes, or until the water has evaporated and the peas have turned into mush.

3 Take the pan off the heat, stir in the butter and the tamarind to taste, then adjust the seasoning if necessary. Serve.

SERVES 4-6

250g (9oz) dried marrowfat peas (if not available use green split peas), soaked overnight in cold water

1½ tbsp sugar, preferably jaggery (palm sugar), but caster sugar is fine

75g (3oz) unsalted butter

1-2 tsp tamarind paste

salt and lots of freshly ground black pepper

This is so, so simple to prepare. If you have any leftovers, leave them in the fridge for a day or two. The flavours will really start to come out and mingle together even more.

Tony's
SPICED RED CABBAGE

1 Heat a large frying pan over a medium-high heat and add the oil. When hot add the cumin seeds and sizzle for 30 seconds, then add the onion and cook for about 10 minutes until soft and golden.

2 Turn up the heat to high, add the cabbage and a few seconds later the butter, and cook for 5 minutes, stirring regularly or tossing to coat the cabbage well; you want it to wilt and soften slightly but retain a bit of crunch, so do not overcook. Add the sugar and the lemon or lime juice, and toss. Season to taste with salt and some pepper, if you like, and serve.

SERVES 6

2 tbsp rapeseed oil or vegetable oil
1 tsp cumin seeds
1 red onion, chopped
½ red cabbage, thinly shredded
1 tbsp butter
1 heaped tsp brown sugar or demerara sugar
1 tsp lemon or lime juice
salt and freshly ground pepper

Mash – one of my favourites. Chilli – super duper. What more is there to say? This mash and the red cabbage opposite go so well with the gammon on page 123 it's unreal.

Tony's
GREEN CHĪLLĪ MASH

1 Preheat the oven to 180°C/350°F/gas 4. With a small sharp knife, pierce the potatoes in few places. Bake in the preheated oven for 1–1½ hours or until tender. Leave to cool slightly.

2 Cut each potato in half and scoop the flesh out. Mash as fine as you can, either with a ricer or just with a fork.

3 Transfer the mash to a pan. Over a low heat, add the butter and cream and blend well to your preferred consistency. Stir in the chilli and salt to taste, and mix well. Serve hot.

SERVES 6

1.5 kg (3lb) baking potatoes, skin on
75g (3oz) butter
75–100ml (2½–3½fl oz) double cream
2 mild fresh green chillies, seeds removed, very finely chopped
salt

A real childhood favourite, this one, but jazzed up a little with the addition of green chillies and a crunchy topping. The heat isn't too overpowering here, but you can play with the amount of chillies either way to get it just to your liking.

Tony's

CAULIFLOWER AND CHILLI CHEESE

1 Preheat the oven to 200°C/400°F/gas 6. Pour the milk into a large saucepan, add the bay leaves, garlic, cloves and cinnamon stick, and bring to the boil. Add the cauliflower florets, leaves and stalks, and simmer for 8–10 minutes until tender but still holding together.

2 Gently lift out the cooked cauliflower with a slotted spoon, removing the bay leaves and cinnamon stick, and set in a colander to drain. Strain the hot milk through a sieve into a jug and reserve.

3 To make the sauce, melt the butter in a medium-size pan over a low heat, then stir in the flour. Stir continuously over a low heat for 2–3 minutes, then gradually add the reserved hot milk, stirring with a whisk so that the sauce is smooth. Bring to a simmer and reduce the heat to very low, then simmer very gently for 5–10 minutes until the flour is cooked out, whisking occasionally.

4 Add the cream and heat the mixture through, then remove from the heat, stir in the Cheddar and whisk until all the cheese has melted. Season generously with salt and pepper. Gently stir the cauliflower into the cheese sauce so that all is well covered, and transfer to an ovenproof dish measuring about 30 x 20cm (12 x 8in).

5 Mix all of the spice topping ingredients together and sprinkle on top of the dish. Bake in the oven for about 20 minutes until golden and bubbling. If you like an extra-crispy topping, flash the dish under a preheated grill for a few minutes before serving.

SERVES 4–6 AS A SIDE DISH

1 litre (1¾ pints) milk
2 bay leaves
1 garlic clove, lightly crushed
2 cloves
3cm (1¼in) piece cinnamon stick
1 cauliflower (about 800g/
   1lb 14oz), cut into florets,
   leaves and stalks reserved

FOR THE SAUCE

60g (2½oz) butter
60g (2½oz) plain flour
100ml (3½fl oz) double cream
120g (4½oz) mature Cheddar,
   grated
salt and freshly ground
   black pepper

FOR THE SPICED TOPPING

50g (2oz) white breadcrumbs
50g (2oz) mature Cheddar,
   grated
30g (1¼oz) Parmesan,
   finely grated
25g (1oz) cornflakes
2 mild fresh green chillies,
   seeds removed if liked,
   finely chopped
1 tbsp finely chopped fresh
   coriander
1 tbsp finely chopped fresh mint

I picked this up when I was in Australia, and it's one of my favourites. I love the crispy crunch of the cabbage, carrot and spring onion, and the fish sauce and chilli round it all off with a punch. It's fantastic.

Tony's
PEANUT & MINT SLAW

1 Put all of the ingredients for the dressing into a jar, close the lid tightly and shake vigorously to combine. Adjust the seasoning to taste and set aside.

2 In a large bowl, mix together all of the ingredients for the slaw itself; don't add the dressing until ready to serve.

3 Just before you serve, mix the dressing thoroughly into the slaw and transfer to a serving bowl.

SERVES 4

FOR THE DRESSING
2 small garlic cloves, grated
1 red bird's-eye chilli,
    seeds removed if liked,
    very finely chopped
1 tbsp rapeseed oil
2 tbsp lime or lemon juice
2 tbsp caster sugar
2 tbsp smooth peanut butter
1½ tbsp Japanese rice vinegar
1½ tbsp hoisin sauce
½ tbsp Thai fish sauce
1 tsp hot chilli paste (optional)

FOR THE SLAW
½ small white cabbage,
    shredded
¾ large carrot, grated
50g (2oz) mooli or English
    radish, grated
6-8 spring onions, finely sliced
3 tbsp roasted peanuts
1 tbsp chopped fresh mint

A delicious coleslaw, that goes perfectly with the rich, meaty flavours of the pulled pork on page 130. This is inspired by the flavours of Goa, and you could pronounce it the way that the Goan cooks used to: 'COALISHLAW!'

Cyrus's

CORIANDER COALISHLAW

1 To make the coleslaw, soak the prepared carrot, cabbage, radish and beetroot for 30 minutes in a large bowl of chilled water with some ice. Drain (the ice will have melted) and leave in a colander to dry off a bit. This will make the vegetables nice and crisp, and prevent them from going too soggy, but if you are short of time you can skip this step.

2 Add the green pepper to the vegetables. In a separate bowl large enough to take all the coleslaw ingredients, mix together the chilli, garlic, coriander, mayonnaise and mustard. Season with salt to taste. Add the crisp, drained vegetables and mix well.

SERVES 4

1 large carrot, finely grated
½ small white cabbage,
    very finely shredded
3 radishes, finely grated
1 small beetroot, finely grated
½ green pepper, seeds removed,
    finely shredded
1 fresh green chilli, seeds
    removed if liked, very finely
    chopped
1 garlic clove, finely crushed
1 heaped tbsp chopped fresh
    coriander
5 heaped tbsp mayonnaise
1½ tbsp English mustard
salt

Tony's
SPICE FOCUS CORIANDER

The name 'coriander' comes from a Greek word meaning 'bug', because there is thought to be a connection between the plant's smell and that of bedbugs! By virtue of its ancient history, coriander might well be one of the oldest flavourings in the world.

The coriander plant is both spice and herb. It is a member of the same family as parsley, cumin, dill and fennel, all native to southern Europe and western Asia. They all grow similarly, with umbels of flowers (like umbrellas), which later set to seed. Commercially the seeds of coriander are collected when they turn from green to a light brown, then they are dried. Seeds that are grown in tropical environments tend to be larger and oval in shape; European and North African seeds are smaller and round.

Coriander is a major crop in India. The seeds – which are little bombs of flavour, warm, sweet, spicy and orangey, but not hot – are valued medicinally by some, as well as in cooking. Lightly toast first in a dry pan to bring out their fragrance, then grind them to a powder. Add to meat or vegetable curries, curry powders and masalas, and to give a last-minute flavouring lift to many dishes, along with freshly ground cumin.

The spice is used in many spice mixes, and can flavour chutneys and pickles, as well as fruit dishes. Add whole seeds to stocks and marinades and, crushed, to add interest to a fish batter, to a bread or biscuit dough, or to root vegetables. Its flavour is especially good with fish, seeds or leaf, and I think you will find it in almost every fish dish in this book! As a child, I used to have to pick through the coriander seeds we had bought, to get rid of the stones and other rubbish. It was actually quite a peaceful job when it was wet outside, but it became a boring chore as soon as the sun was shining and my friends were out playing...

Fresh coriander is classified as a herb, so probably doesn't have a place here, but I couldn't cook without it. When I was small, we had to travel to Glasgow from Leith to buy it before my mum started growing it in the garden. If you like it (many people don't), add at the last minute to dishes. Use the roots as well, which are highly flavoured. My mum used to make a chutney with liquidised leaves and roots, ginger, chilli and garlic; we took this on picnics, eating it with home-made bread. Once upon a time, when you bought a good amount of vegetables from an Indian stallholder, he would throw in a free bunch of fresh coriander (those were the days). Put the bunch, usually with roots intact, in a jug of water in the fridge, and it will keep for a day or so. The leaves are very rich in vitamin C, and if I'm in the mood for a bit of a change I throw them into many dishes as an alternative to parsley.

While we were on holiday recently in Forli, Italy, my old friend Dr Ferdinando Romano invited us over for what he said would be some simple food and potatoes *al forno* (cooked in the oven). When we arrived we discovered that he had been so excited we were coming that he had forgotten to cook! We caught up on old gossip and drank a little Cinzano, then rapidly put together this dish with the potatoes he'd bought and whatever we found, and it turned out just great.

Cyrus
FERDINANDO'S ROASTED POTATOES

1 Preheat the oven to 180°C/350°F/gas 4. Place all of the ingredients except the tomatoes in a roasting tin and mix well. Cook in the hot oven for 20 minutes, then mix well again, level out and return to the oven for a further 10 minutes. Check that the potatoes are fully cooked and tinged golden-brown; if not, cook for a further 5–10 minutes.

2 Add the sliced tomato to the dish and mix gently, then return the dish to the oven for 5 minutes. Turn off the oven but leave the dish to rest for 5 minutes before serving. Eat the potatoes with some cheese and slices of charcuterie, as we did, as an accompaniment to a meal or simply on its own.

NOTE: You can also sprinkle some good grated cheese on the top after cooking; the cheese will melt while the dish is resting in the oven.

SERVES 4

1kg (2lb 4oz) potatoes, peeled, quartered and sliced to approximately 3mm (⅛in) thickness
4 garlic cloves, chopped
1 fresh red chilli, seeds removed, chopped
1 tsp cumin seeds, crushed
½ tsp finely chopped fresh rosemary
5 tbsp olive oil
2 medium firm tomatoes, cut into sixths
salt and freshly ground black pepper

Our minds are set to the traditional and must be exposed to different flavours gradually, so I haven't gone overboard in this variation on the traditional Yorkshire pud – I do encourage you to play about with the recipe as you get used to the flavours! For the best results measure out your flour in a measuring jug , as you need the same volume of flour, milk and eggs – it may seem a little strange to do it this way but trust me, it works.

Cyrus's

SPICED YORKSHIRE PUDDING

1 Pour the eggs and milk into a mixing bowl and add some salt. Whisk thoroughly with an electric beater or balloon whisk, add the chopped green chilli and whisk again. Leave to stand for 10 minutes.

2 Sift the flour and chilli powder into the egg mixture, and whisk once more to create a lump-free batter resembling thick cream. (If there are any lumps, pass the batter through a fine sieve, remembering to put the chillies back in the batter.)

3 Leave the batter to rest at room temperature for at least 30 minutes, and longer if possible. If you have the time, after resting the batter refrigerate it for several hours, as a cold batter generally achieves the best results. Meanwhile, preheat the oven to high, but do not exceed 230°C/450°F/gas 8 as the fat will burn and splatter around the oven, creating a mess and a nasty smell in the kitchen.

4 Put a 12-hole muffin tin or Yorkshire pudding tin (with 10 x 5cm/ 4 x 2in holes) into the oven for a few minutes to heat through, then remove and add small drizzle of oil or a pea-sized piece of lard or dripping to each hole, and heat the tin again in the oven until the fat is smoking.

5 Whisk the batter a final time, adding 2 tbsp cold water, and transfer to a large jug so that it's easier to pour. Fill one third of each hole in the tin with batter, sprinkle with black pepper and return the tin to the oven immediately. Cook for 20 minutes or until well risen and golden brown.

MAKES 12–15 PUDDINGS

4 eggs, lightly whisked (total volume about 200ml/7fl oz)
milk (same volume as eggs, about 200ml/7fl oz)
1 green bird's-eye chilli, seeds removed if liked, very finely chopped
plain flour (same volume as eggs, about 200ml/7fl oz)
1 tsp chilli powder
2–3 tbsp rapeseed oil, vegetable oil, lard or dripping
salt and freshly ground black pepper

I have a jar of this in my fridge at all times, no exceptions. You can use it for so much! It's perfect as a condiment, you can put it in recipes that need a lift, it goes well in sandwiches, or anything else that you can think of. Or you can try my guilty pleasure if you want a quick snack – pile it up on some prawn crackers.

Tony's
SPĪCED PĪCKLED ONĪONS

1 Put all of the ingredients except the tarragon and coriander in a sterilised sealable glass jar with a capacity of 750ml–1 litre (1 pint 7fl oz–1¾ pints).

2 Give it a good mix, seal and leave for at least 3 hours, shaking the jar every now and then. The onions are best if kept for a week before serving; again, shake the jar from time to time. When serving, garnish with a little chopped coriander and tarragon. The onions go well with the Goat's Cheese, Red Onion and Caraway Seed Tart (see page 30).

MAKES 500G
500g (1lb 2oz) red onions, finely sliced
juice of 2 limes
2 tbsp distilled vinegar
chilli flakes, to taste
1½ tbsp pomegranate molasses
chopped tarragon and coriander, to serve

British apples and pears can make superb chutneys, as I've learned over the past few years. My favourite apples for chutneys are Russets, Bramleys and Braeburns; with pears I am not selective, they are all good. The pectin here gives a satisfying firm set, but the recipe will work without it, too. This chutney is fab as a glaze for roast chicken and pork, and also makes a great accompaniment to cheese. If you follow the instructions below it will keep in a cool, dark place for a year.

Cyrus's
APPLE AND PEAR CHUTNEY

1 In a heavy-bottomed pan large enough to contain all the ingredients comfortably, put the sugar, vinegar and cinnamon and bring slowly to the boil, stirring occasionally. Meanwhile, wash and dry the fruit. Core them and cut into 2cm (¾in) pieces.

2 When the syrup comes to boil and the sugar has dissolved, add the chilli, salt and cut fruit and bring back to the boil. When the fruit starts to cook and the chutney bubbles rather than boils, stir well to break up the fruit and add the chopped peppers. Simmer for about 1½ hours until the chutney thickens, stirring from time to time.

3 Taste the chutney – cool the spoonful first as boiling chutneys and jams retain latent heat and can be very hot. Add more salt if you wish, then stir in the pectin, if using. Remove the cinnamon and chilli with tongs.

4 Pour the chutney into hot sterilised jars, filling them up to the neck as cleanly as possible, and seal the jars immediately. Leave to cool. Allow the chutney to rest for a week before eating.

MAKES 6 X 450G JARS

1kg (2lb 4oz) preserving sugar
250ml (9fl oz) cider vinegar
10cm (4in) cinnamon stick,
    broken into three pieces
1kg (2lb 4oz) apples
    (about 6 apples)
1kg (2lb 4oz) pears
    (about 7 pears)
1 red chilli, bashed
    with a rolling pin
2 green peppers, very finely
    chopped
3 tbsp pectin (optional)
6 jars with lids, cleaned and
    then sterilised in the oven
    at 140°C/275°/gas 1
2 tsp salt

Cyrus's
CIDER
BREWING
SOMERSET

I don't think we make cider in India
with our apples, but what a good idea
it would be: cider is one of the best
accompaniments for Indian food. Beers
and selected wines, such as those from
Alsace, are good with curries, but the
cider that we tasted at Roger Wilkins'
Cider Farm in Somerset had just the
right levels of acidity, and would be
perfect. (Actually, thinking about it,
India would be more likely to make an
eau de vie from apples or apple juice –
they'd distil anything there!)

Neither Tony or I was a particular fan
of cider until we tasted Roger's wares.
He has been producing cider since he
was a boy, has an orchard with some
300 apple trees and an apple press
dating from 1868.

After our tasting, I cooked a gammon,
adding cinnamon, red chillies and
coriander seeds to the cider braising
liquid, along with apple juice and
apples – just to intensify that wonderful
flavour. I then glazed the gammon, after
trimming off the rind, and roasted it. It
was delicious, even without the cloves
which decorate most baked hams: such
a waste of precious cloves, as they are
flavouring the fat, not the meat.

You might think apples and gammon
or ham are not very Indian, but we
have both. Ham was introduced by the
Portuguese, and the Goans in particular

have been making ham for centuries. It is known as *presunto*, the Portuguese word for ham. In Goa we boil gammon very similarly, but probably using more potent spices such as cloves, perhaps cassia or star anise, with a few *tej-pat* leaves (also known as Indian bay leaves). Pork, as I have said before, can take such powerful spicing.

While we were at Roger's farm, we made a mulled cider, with added nutmeg, cinnamon and ground ginger. You could do much the same with a nice British ale. Mulled wine – usually red wine heated gently with spices – has been traditional in Britain for centuries, perhaps even dating from Roman times. It's certainly popular in the wintertime, at Hallowe'en and Christmas. The spices are usually cloves, nutmeg, mace and cinnamon. You could also try Tony's Spiced Buttered Rum, (see page 240) with its intense flavours coming from cardamom, nutmeg, cloves, vanilla and an aromatic and slightly unusual stirrer – a cinnamon stick.

But the spiced drink most familiar to Indians, and increasingly in the West, is masala chai, or spiced tea. Although the Portuguese were drinking tea long before the British, it was the British who began the commercial production of tea on the subcontinent. We have since taken to it as enthusiastically as we did to the chilli. Black tea is infused with spices, often with (buffalo) milk and sugar (or condensed milk) as well. The spices can vary, often according to their medicinal qualities, but on the whole cardamom is predominant, followed closely by ground ginger, with some chais flavoured by cinnamon, star anise, peppercorns, cloves and fennel seeds. But even the simplest spiced tea can do you good. My mum used to put ginger peelings on the windowsill to dry. The next morning she made a tea from them, and we'd be full of zing all day!

DESSERTS

& A FEW WEE DRINKS

Originally, the traditional Scottish cranachan celebrated the harvest, but now it is enjoyed year-round. There are many variations, but in all of them the trick is the slow toasting of the oatmeal; this is then mixed into the dish at the last minute so that its texture is retained. The quantities given here for the cardamom honey make a full jar, much more than you need for this amount of cranachan, but it will keep indefinitely; it is great over granola and in coffee.

Tony's
SCOTTISH CRANACHAN WITH A WEE TWIST

1 To make the Cardamom Honey, pour half of the honey into a pan and add the cardamom. Gently heat through until the honey has become more liquid and starts to bubble at the edges; if you have a probe thermometer, the temperature should be 75°F (165°F). Remove from the heat and pour the flavoured honey back into the jar with the remaining honey. Stir gently, and leave to cool, uncovered. When cool, put on the lid and ideally store for 24 hours before using.

2 To make the cranachan, heat a heavy-bottomed pan and toast the oatmeal over a lowish heat, stirring occasionally, until it smells warm and nutty and has changed colour; this will take 10–15 minutes, sometimes as long as 20 minutes. Leave to cool.

3 In a bowl, crush half of the raspberries to make a rough mash. In a separate bowl, whisk the cream with the honey, whisky and rose water until soft peaks form, then fold in the crushed raspberries.

4 Fold in the toasted oatmeal and two-thirds of the remaining whole raspberries. Adjust the honey and rose water to taste. Spoon the cranachan into small glasses, and garnish with the remaining raspberries and some rose petals, if using. Drizzle with a wee bit more of the Cardamom Honey and serve.

SERVES 4–6
40g (1½oz) medium
   or coarse oatmeal
200g (7oz) raspberries
400ml (14fl oz) double cream
2 tbsp Cardamom Honey
   (below), or to taste
3 tbsp malt whisky
½–1 tsp rose water, or to taste
rose petals, to garnish (optional)

FOR THE CARDAMOM HONEY
1 x 250g (9oz) jar clear honey
1 tsp ground cardamom
   (about 24 cardamom pods,
   seeds finely ground)

Sometimes I find bread and butter pudding a little bit heavy. The addition of orange here cuts through the rib-sticking bread and makes things a little lighter, and the cardamom brings a perfumed flavour that works perfectly with the orange.

Tony's

BREAD & BUTTER PUDDING WITH ORANGE & CARDAMOM

1 Remove the zest from the oranges and set the rest of the oranges aside. Pour the milk and cream into a pan, add the orange zest, split vanilla pod and crushed cardamoms and bring to the boil. Turn off the heat and leave to infuse for 1 hour.

2 Preheat the oven to 180°C/350°F/gas 4 and place a large roasting tin inside to warm up – the tin should be large enough to hold the baking dish (see step 4) with space remaining around the edge.

3 Butter the bread and cut it into triangles. Segment the oranges with a sharp knife and discard the peel. Remove the translucent outer skin from each segment, and discard. Slice each segment in half. Beat the eggs and sugar together in a mixing bowl. Pour the infused milk through a fine sieve onto the egg mixture.

4 Arrange a layer of bread, buttered-side up, in a 30 x 22 x 5cm (12 x 9 x 2in) ovenproof dish, then add a layer of pistachio pieces, sultanas and orange segments. Repeat the layers, finishing with the bread and making the final layer overlap neatly. Pour the milk-and-egg mixture over the top. Put on a kettle of water to boil.

5 Place the dish in the roasting tin in the oven. Carefully pour boiling water into the roasting tin to come halfway up the sides of the dish, taking care not to allow any of the water to go into the pudding. Bake for 30–40 minutes until nearly set through.

6 Heat the marmalade in a small pan over gentle heat until liquid, and use to brush the top of the bread and butter pudding with the marmalade. To serve, scoop out each portion and dust with icing sugar, plus a dollop of crème fraîche if you like.

SERVES 6–8
3 oranges
300ml (½ pint) milk
300ml (½ pint) double cream
1 vanilla pod, split
15 green cardamom pods, crushed with a pestle and mortar
90g (3½oz) butter, softened
15 slices bread, preferably slightly stale
8 eggs
175g (6oz) caster sugar
55g (2oz) shelled pistachios, chopped
85g (3¼oz) golden sultanas
4 tbsp Seville orange marmalade, peel removed

TO SERVE
icing sugar
crème fraîche (optional)

A lovely traditional pudding, but the *star* of the show – see what I've done there? – is the star anise, which gives the dish a warming, aromatic feel. But it's the crunchy, twice-cooked crumble topping that really does it for me. Once you've tried it this way, this is how you'll always make it.

Tony's

APPLE CRUMBLE WITH STAR ANISE

1 Preheat the oven to 200°C/400°F/gas 6. To make the crumble topping, put the flour and brown sugar in a large bowl and mix well. Taking a few cubes of butter at a time, rub them into the flour mixture until it resembles breadcrumbs.

2 Sprinkle the mixture onto a baking sheet in a thin layer, using two sheets if necessary. Bake in the preheated oven for 5 minutes or until lightly golden brown. Remove from the oven and break with a fork, then return to the oven and repeat the process a couple of times, until you have a lovely crunchy biscuit topping. Set aside; if continuing to cook the apple crumble immediately, do not turn the oven off.

3 To make the filling, heat a wide, shallow, heavy-bottomed pan and melt the butter until it foams. Add the apples, sugar, star anise and cinnamon, and cook, stirring frequently, until the sugar has dissolved and the apple is soft at the edges. Remove the cinnamon and the star anise, and add a little bit more sugar if you like.

4 To assemble, butter a medium-sized ovenproof dish. Spoon the fruit mixture into the bottom, then sprinkle the crumble mixture on top. Ensure the oven is preheated to 200°C/400°F/gas 6, and bake for 20 minutes until the crumble is browned and the fruit mixture bubbling. Leave to cool slightly.

5 To serve, put some crème fraîche into a small bowl and mix in some pomegranate seeds. Drizzle with a little pomegranate syrup and serve alongside the crumble.

SERVES 6

FOR THE CRUMBLE TOPPING
300g (10½oz) plain flour
200g (7oz) brown sugar
200g (7oz) unsalted butter, cubed and softened to room temperature, plus extra for greasing
pinch of salt

FOR THE FILLING
75g (3oz) unsalted butter
1 kg (2lb 4oz) eating apples (such as russet or cox), peeled, cored and chopped into large chunks
150g (5oz) caster sugar
5 star anise
1 cinnamon stick

TO SERVE (OPTIONAL)
crème fraîche
pomegranate seeds
pomegranate syrup

SPICE FOCUS
STAR ANISE

Star anise is one of the ingredients of five-spice powder, and is used whole in the slow-cooked and red-cooked dishes of eastern Chinese cooking – and in some of the best spare ribs I have ever had. It features in Indian dishes as well: in stews and curries, ground in garam masala, and in chutneys and teas. I think it adds huge flavour and a real depth to red meats such as beef or oxtail, and can be surprisingly subtle when used with fish.

Also known as Chinese anise, star anise is the fruit of a small evergreen shrub or tree of the magnolia family. It is native to south-west China, and only grows there, in Vietnam and some parts of India.

The tree bears beautiful white flowers which become a fruit, consisting of six to eight carpels arranged in a whorl. When dried the fruit is star-shaped, hard, wrinkled and dark reddish-brown in colour. Each carpel contains a small shiny seed. The spice is the whole fruit, seeds, carpels and all. It is best to buy the whole dried fruit, as this can last, in airtight conditions, for up to a year. You can grind it in a pestle and mortar, or in a spice-grinder, although it will never be as powdery as the ground you can buy. And buy this, if you can find it, sparingly, as the aromatic oils will diminish.

The flavour is very similar to aniseed, though slightly more potent and pungent, with warm notes of liquorice. This flavour is very important in Chinese cuisine and, according to Heston Blumenthal, it transforms the flavour of onions when you're caramelising them. It goes well with other naturally sweet vegetables like pumpkin and roots too, and I also like it in desserts: try some ground in brownie or chocolate cake recipes (a star anise chocolate or toffee would be good), or whole in a fruit-poaching syrup. I use it in a to-die-for apple crumble on page 212), and both Cyrus and I like flavouring our tea with it by warming the milk up on the stove with a couple of whole star anise. This is the influence of my dad, who used to stew his masala chai with star anise. At home we called it 'tinkers' tea' because tinkers stewed their tea for ages as well. Just go easy, though, as a little star anise goes a long way...

Anise, star anise, fennel and liquorice all contain a flavouring chemical compound called anethole. Star anise is now used, instead of anise, in oils and extracts for baking and in alcohols such as Sambuca, Galliano (think Harvey Wallbanger) and pastis. The spice has been used for years in Asia, probably because it's a warming spice: it's been used to treat rheumatism and colds, and is thought by some to be very good for the digestion and even for sweetening your breath!

An apple tatin was one of the first desserts that I cooked for my mum and it's still her favourite. We've replaced the apples with pears here, and served it with an interesting allspice ice cream for you to try – it has a wonderful flavour but isn't too sweet, so goes really well with the sugary tart.

Tony's

PEAR & HONEY TATĪN WĪTH ALLSPĪCE ĪCE CREAM

1 First make the ice cream. Pour the milk and cream into a pan, stir in the allspice and bring to the boil. Meanwhile, beat the yolks and sugar together until the mixture becomes thick, smooth and creamy.

2 Very gradually pour the hot cream mixture through a fine sieve (it needs to be a fine sieve to strain out as much of the allspice as possible) into the sweetened yolk mixture, mixing as you do so. The hot liquid needs to be mixed in slowly at first, to avoid curdling; once half is added, you can add the rest more quickly, mixing well.

3 Return the mixture to a low-medium heat and stir continuously until it starts to thicken so that it coats the back of a spoon; this should take about 10 minutes. Remove from the heat and leave to cool, then refrigerate overnight.

4 Churn the chilled mixture in an ice cream machine, following the manufacturer's instructions. If you don't have an ice cream machine, pour the mixture into a deep, wide dish and put it in the freezer. After 45 minutes, as it's starting to freeze around the edges, remove from the freezer and whisk the mixture thoroughly to break up any frozen pieces. Return to the freezer for 30 minutes and repeat this process. Continue to do this at 30 minute intervals until you have the desired texture.

5 To make the pear and honey tatin, peel the pears, cut them in half lengthways and remove the core.

6 Heat a heavy-based 25cm (10in) ovenproof frying pan over a medium heat. Add the butter, honey and sugar, and heat until smooth and liquid, stirring occasionally to help the sugar dissolve. Then allow to bubble, stirring occasionally, for about 5 minutes until the mixture has coloured to a deep golden brown caramel; don't let it get too dark as it will caramelise a little further during baking.

SERVES 6
6 pears, as ripe as possible
100g (4oz) unsalted butter
100g (4oz) honey
75g (3oz) soft brown sugar
375g (13oz) all-butter puff pastry

FOR THE ALLSPICE ICE CREAM
400ml (14fl oz) milk
400ml (14fl oz) double cream
2 tbsp ground allspice
4 egg yolks
100g (4oz) caster sugar

Continues overleaf

7 Carefully add the pears, cut-side up, to the very hot caramel in the pan, and leave to cool for about 15 minutes. Meanwhile, preheat the oven to 180°C/350°F/gas 4.

8 Roll out the puff pastry to a 5mm (¼in) thick circle slightly larger than the top of the pan. Drape the pastry over the pears and caramel, and tuck it in at the sides so that it goes down the inside of the pan – like tucking in a blanket. Bake for about 40 minutes until the pastry is completely cooked.

9 Remove the tatin from the oven and leave to cool in the pan for 5 minutes. Turn out the tatin by placing a deep-sided plate or shallow dish over the pan and carefully (using oven gloves as the pan will still be hot) flip the pan over. You need to be really careful when you do this, as if the pears are particularly juicy then some hot juice may spill out as you flip the pan. If you cool the tatin for too long before turning it out the caramel will set and everything will stick to the pan; if this happens, set the pan over a low heat for a minute to just soften the caramel. Serve the tatin warm, topped with the ice cream.

We love this classic British pudding. Here we've added ginger and cinnamon sticks to the pudding to give it a bit of a lift – it turns it into a real winter warmer of a pud. We've used fresh breadcrumbs too but, as this dessert was traditionally made to use up old bread, it will work nicely with stale bread or even cake crumbs.

Tony's

GINGER QUEEN OF PUDDINGS

1 Preheat the oven to 180°C/350°F/gas 4 and put a roasting tin in the oven to warm. Grease a 15cm (6in) diameter ovenproof dish with butter.

2 Pour the milk into a pan over a low heat and add the 50g (2oz) butter, the cinnamon and 1 tablespoon of the sugar. Bring slowly to the boil, stirring occasionally, and cook till the milk is reduced by roughly one-fifth to 200ml (7fl oz); this should take about 5 minutes of boiling.

3 Put the breadcrumbs in a bowl and pour the hot milk mixture all over, then allow to soak for 5 minutes; meanwhile, put a kettle on to boil. Stir the lime zest and juice into the soaked breadcrumbs, then the beaten egg yolks.

4 Pour the mixture into the prepared ovenproof dish. Set the dish in the roasting tin in the oven, and carefully pour boiling water into the roasting tin to come halfway up the sides of the pudding dish. Bake for 20–25 minutes until firmly set.

5 When the pudding is cooked, remove it from the oven and allow it to cool in its dish. Warm the ginger preserve then spread evenly over the pudding.

6 To make the meringue topping, preheat the oven back to 180°C/350°F/gas 4. Whisk the egg whites until soft peaks form, then gradually add the remaining sugar and whisk until smooth and glossy. Spread this over the pudding, swirling it into peaks. Return the dish to the oven and bake for 15–20 minutes, or until the meringue is lightly browned on top. Serve straight away.

SERVES 4
250ml (9fl oz) milk
50g (2oz) butter, plus extra for greasing
15cm (6in) stick cinnamon, broken into small bits
100g (4oz) caster sugar
100g (4oz) fresh white breadcrumbs
grated zest and juice of 2 limes
2 eggs, separated, yolks lightly beaten
125g (4½oz) ginger preserve

We wanted to put a nice treacle pudding in the book, and after we visited a traditional sweet shop in Wales, coming up with this nutmeg-infused recipe was a no-brainer. The treacle toffee melts to give you a lovely, rich topping – delicious drizzled with some toffee sauce. If you're short on time, you can also make four smaller, individual puddings by steaming them in the oven (see the note below).

Tony's

TREACLE PUDDING WITH NUTMEG, LEMON & LIME

1 Bring a large pan of water to the boil and place a steamer on top. (You will also need a lid.) Cream the butter and sugar together with an electric beater until pale and fluffy.

2 Add half of the beaten eggs and continue to beat for 1–2 minutes. Stop, scrape the sides of the bowl, then add the remaining beaten egg and continue beating for 1–2 minutes. Scrape the sides again. Add the nutmeg, lime and lemon zest, and beat for a few seconds more.

3 With a metal spoon, gradually fold the sifted flour and baking powder into the mixture as lightly as you can, keeping to a dropping consistency by adding milk, if needed. Fold in the toffee or fudge pieces.

4 Butter and lightly flour a 1.2 litre (2 pint) pudding basin. Spoon the treacle into the bottom of the basin, then add the pudding mixture. Secure the lid and steam gently for 3 hours, adding more water to the pan if necessary – keep a close eye on the pan so it doesn't boil dry. The pudding is cooked when a skewer inserted into it comes out clean.

5 If you want to make some extra sauce, melt a couple of toffees or pieces of fudge in a small saucepan along with a splash of water. When the toffee starts to melt, stir in a glug of double cream. Warm through until the toffee has melted and pour over the pudding to serve.

NOTE: For four individual puddings, preheat the oven to 180°C/350°F/ gas 4 and butter and flour four ovenproof ramekins as above. Divide the treacle between the ramekins, then do the same with the pudding mixture. Place the dishes in a deep roasting tin, pour boiling water into the tin until it comes half way up the sides of the ramekins, then put the tin in the oven for 40 minutes, until a skewer inserted comes out clean.

SERVES 4

85g (3¼oz) butter, well softened, plus extra for greasing
115g (4¼oz) caster sugar
2 eggs, lightly beaten
1 nutmeg, grated
grated zest of 1 lime
grated zest of 1 lemon
140g (4¾oz) self-raising flour, sifted, plus extra for dusting
1 tsp baking powder
1 tbsp milk, or more if needed
55g (2oz) treacle toffee (if not available, use butterscotch or fudge), chopped into small pieces, plus extra for the sauce (optional)
3 tbsp treacle

FOR THE SAUCE
a few pieces treacle toffee
splash double cream

A classic Victoria Sponge, with a difference – or let's just say it's slightly twisted! You too should try using the vast amounts of spices and flavours at your disposal to work in different ideas to gently twist classic dishes.

Cyrus's
VICTORIA SPONGE WITH FENNEL

1 Preheat the oven to 190°C/375°F/gas 5. Grease two 20cm (8in) sandwich tins with butter, and line the bottoms with baking parchment.

2 Using an electric beater or a wooden spoon, beat together the salted butter and caster sugar until light and fluffy. Mix in the eggs a little at a time, then fold in the flour, baking powder and ground cardamom. Add the cream or milk to loosen the batter.

3 Spoon out evenly into the two tins, level the surface and bake for about 20 minutes until firm but springy to the touch. Remove from the oven and turn out onto a wire rack; peel off the baking parchment.

4 To make the buttercream filling, use an electric beater or wooden spoon to cream the butter well until light and fluffy. Beat in the icing sugar a little at a time, adding the milk or water to loosen the mixture. Add the orange zest and crushed fennel seeds and continue to beat until the flavours are well blended.

5 Taste the orange juice; if it's a bit sour, add a little icing sugar to sweeten. With a fork, poke holes in the base of each cake and pour the juice over both. Spread the buttercream over one cake, and the marmalade over the other. Sandwich the two together, dust the top with icing sugar and serve.

NOTE: You could of course dry-fry the fennel seeds in a frying pan before grinding them as finely as you can with a pestle and mortar. Alternatively, once the cakes are cooked you can toast the seeds on a baking tray as soon as you've turned the oven off; it will take only a few minutes.

SERVES 8
200g (7oz) salted butter, softened, plus extra for greasing
200g (7oz) caster sugar
4 eggs, beaten
200g (7oz) plain flour
2 tsp baking powder
1 tsp ground cardamom (about 24 cardamom pods, seeds finely ground)
4 tsp cream or milk
3–4 tbsp sweet orange marmalade

FOR THE BUTTERCREAM FILLING
140g (4¾oz) unsalted butter, softened
140g (4¾oz) icing sugar, sifted
1 tbsp milk or water
finely grated zest and juice of 1 small orange
1 tsp fennel seeds, toasted and ground

The people of Bombay love their puddings, and this one was popular when I was little. Most bakeries, after the morning batch of bread was done, would bake standard Madeira-style cakes in the ovens as the wood was burning out. The bakers then trimmed off the sides (Indians will not eat the crust of bread or cake as they feel they are being cheated), and the trimmings went into this yummy pudding, which for some reason got named 'cabinet pudding' – don't ask me why!

Cyrus's

BOMBAY-STYLE CABINET PUDDING

1 Pour the milk into a deep casserole dish and bring to the boil, then reduce the heat and let the milk simmer for 25–30 minutes, taking care not to let it boil over, until reduced to about 1 litre (1¾ pints). Check that the milk has reduced correctly by carefully pouring it into a measuring jug. Don't worry if it has reduced to a little less than 1 litre. Leave to cool slightly.

2 Meanwhile, preheat the oven to 140°C/275°F/gas 1. Butter a 30 x 23cm (12 x 9in) baking dish, then sprinkle with 1 tablespoon of the sugar and rotate the dish, spreading the sugar evenly. Place in the oven a large roasting tin that will hold the baking dish, with at least 1cm (½in) around the edge.

3 Cut the Madeira sponge into 1cm (½in) slices. Place these in the baking dish and press down firmly, then dot with the raspberry jam.

4 Whisk together the remaining sugar and the eggs, then gradually add the warm (not hot) milk, whisking continuously to prevent any coagulation. (Use a stick blender if you have one, as it is very efficient and creates a smooth mix.)

5 Beat the ground cardamom into the mixture and taste. If it does not taste sweet enough for your liking, before adding more sugar ask yourself whether the sugar in the cake and the baking dish itself, and the jam, might make the pudding sweet enough. Indians, who love things really sweet, will want to add sugar for sure, but you might not agree. Pour the mix over the cake pieces and jam, and soak for 5 minutes. Meanwhile, boil a kettle of water.

6 Cover the pudding with aluminium foil. Place the dish in the preheated roasting tin, and carefully pour boiling water into the roasting tin so that it comes roughly 2cm (¾in) up the sides of the baking dish. Bake for 35 minutes, then check if the centre of the pudding is cooked

SERVES 6-8

1.2 litres (2 pints) milk
butter for greasing, plus extra
   for melting
3 tbsp caster sugar,
   or more to taste
300g (10½oz) plain Madeira
   sponge
6 tbsp raspberry jam
4 eggs
½ tsp ground cardamom
   (about 12 cardamom pods,
   seeds finely ground)
double cream, to serve (optional)

by inserting a skewer or a thin knife, which should come out clean. Generally the pudding will need some 10 minutes more baking (45 minutes in total), but it's always good to check: if you continue baking after the pudding is fully cooked, the custard will develop a poor texture and the pudding will sink in the middle.

7 When the pudding is cooked, remove it from the oven and gently brush with melted butter (don't smear, as the pudding is fragile and will break up), then grill until golden. Alternatively, if you want to give the pudding a thicker crust, allow it to cool completely, then smear some butter on the top and flash the pudding under the grill (I really like this, as a little crust adds a super flavour). Serve warm or cold, with some cream if you like.

To be honest, the figs and the cake aren't the main attraction here – it's all about that lovely syrup. The nutmeg is so warming and sits very well with the nuttiness of the fig seeds, and the Rioja cake is delicious and rich too but, for me, they're just there to soak up the juices!

Tony's

RĪOJA CAKE WĪTH NUTMEG FĪGS & SPĪCED CREAM

1 Preheat the oven to 180°C/350°F/gas 4. Generously butter 6 dariole moulds of 175ml (6fl oz) capacity.

2 In a mixing bowl, beat the butter and sugar together until light and fluffy. Beat the egg yolks into the mixture one at a time. Gently stir in the warm wine. Sift the dry ingredients together then fold into the mixture.

3 Whisk the egg whites to stiff peaks. Mix a quarter into the cake mix to slacken, then gently fold in the rest.

4 Spoon the mixture into the dariole moulds and bake for 20 minutes or until risen and a skewer inserted in the middle comes out clean. Meanwhile, start making the poaching syrup for the figs. Place all of the poached spice fig ingredients except for the figs themselves into a heavy-bottomed pan. Add 200ml (7fl oz) of water, bring to the boil and boil for 15 minutes.

5 When the cakes have cooked, leave them to cool for a few minutes, then remove from the tins but keep warm.

6 Strain the syrup for the figs through a sieve into a clean pan, crushing the blackcurrants against the sides. Taste for sweetness and add more sugar if needed. Add the figs and simmer gently for 5 minutes or until tender. Meanwhile, to make the spiced cream, beat the cream and spices together until soft peaks form.

7 Take the figs off the heat. If the syrup is too thin, remove the figs and return the liquid to a high heat heat and boil until reduced to the consistency of cordial. Serve the cakes warm, with the warm poached figs, plenty of the poaching syrup and a generous dollop of spiced cream.

MAKES 6

125g (4½oz) butter, softened, plus extra for greasing
75g (3oz) light brown sugar
3 eggs, separated
500ml (17fl oz) Rioja, reduced to 60ml (2¼fl oz) by boiling in a large pan for 15–20 minutes, cooled but still warm
150g (5oz) plain flour
¾ tsp baking powder
1 tbsp cocoa powder
¼ tsp ground cinnamon

FOR THE POACHED SPICED FIGS

200ml (7fl oz) Rioja
400ml (14fl oz) port
½ nutmeg, grated
175g (6oz) granulated sugar
250g (9oz) blackcurrants (fresh or frozen)
9 ripe figs, cut in half

FOR THE SPICED CREAM

175ml (6fl oz) double cream
seeds from ½ a vanilla pod
¼ nutmeg, grated, or to taste

The rice puddings that are so popular in Britain have been adopted from the Indian subcontinent, where they are eaten at room temperature or cold during the hot summer months as they have a cooling effect on the stomach after a heavy meal. This is a rather rich pudding, bringing together the flavours of such spices as cardamom and cinnamon, and the option of saffron as an extra touch; this simple recipe brings oodles of flavour to the common-or-garden rice pudding.

Cyrus's

RICE PUDDING, PARSEE-STYLE

1 With a pestle and mortar, or with the hilt of a chopper, bruise the cardamom pods until they pop and the seeds inside loosen. Heat a casserole dish or saucepan on a medium heat, add the cardamom pods and cinnamon or cassia, and toast, stirring occasionally, for 2–3 minutes. Add the butter and continue to cook the two spices until swelled a bit.

2 Add the rice, stir to coat, and add 100ml (3½fl oz) of water. Stir over a medium heat until the water has been absorbed, then add 800ml (1 pint 9fl oz) milk and continue to cook at a low simmer for around 20–25 minutes or until the rice is tender. Stir well and scrape the sides clean with a spatula regularly; a flat wooden spatula is best in case the rice sticks at the bottom. The cooked consistency should be quite runny, so add more milk if you need to during cooking.

3 Add 20g (¾oz) of the sugar, the sultanas and a small pinch of salt, and simmer for 2–3 minutes, again ensuring the mixture contains a good amount of liquid, as the dish will thicken as it cools. Taste, and add more sugar if you wish, simmering briefly to allow it to dissolve. Turn off the heat and cover with a lid to prevent a skin forming, and allow to cool to room temperature.

4 When ready to serve, add the rose water and the vanilla essence, if using, and mix well. Spoon into a large serving bowl or into individual bowls, and sprinkle with the slivered almonds or pistachios.

NOTE: For a special occasion, sprinkling saffron strands on top of the pudding when serving adds an extra flavour to the dish.

SERVES 4

4 green or white cardamom pods
5cm (2in) cinnamon stick or cassia bark
20g (¾oz) unsalted butter
100g (4oz) basmati rice, washed well and drained
800ml–1 litre (1 pint 9fl oz– 1¾ pints) milk
20–40g (¾–1½oz) caster sugar, or to taste
75g (3oz) sultanas, long light-green ones if available
½ tsp rose water
¼ tsp vanilla extract (optional)
6 almonds, blanched and slivered, or pistachios, roughly chopped
a few saffron strands, gently toasted in a dry frying pan and soaked in 1 tsp warm water or milk (optional)
salt

SPICE FOCUS
CARDAMOM

Cardamom is my favourite spice. The first thing to get your head around is that there are several types of cardamom. The one that is most valued – 'the queen of spices' – is green cardamom, *Elettaria*; black cardamom comes from a related plant, *Amomum*. Both are native to India and Sri Lanka, and belong to the ginger family. Guatemala is now the world's largest producer of the spice, which is amazing, as the plant was only introduced from India a few years before the First World War.

Green cardamom grows on a large bush which likes shady conditions, so is often grown in coffee plantations. The small seed pods are oval, picked when light green in colour (white ones will have been bleached). Each pod contains rows of dark seeds; these are the spice, their flavour and aroma warm, lemony and flowery all at the same time. Cyrus says raw fresh cardamom pods, eaten whole, are incredibly sweet.

Black cardamom has much larger pods that are red when ripe, dark brown when dried, and very hairy! The seeds are larger too, and their flavour is more astringent, smoky and earthy than green cardamom. It is often sold, ground, as a cheaper substitute for green cardamom.

The small greenish unbleached pods are the most valued in Indian cooking; they are used whole or crushed in curries, pilaus, and ground in many curry powders, and almost every garam masala blend. Black cardamoms are used similarly. In Arab countries, green cardamom is ground with coffee beans, or crushed pods are stuffed into the spout of the coffee pot.

The green variety is used most in sweet dishes in India, and this is where we have mounted our main cardamom assault: it's in my cranachan on page 209, in our bread and butter and cabinet puddings (see page 210 and 228) and homemade honeycomb (see page 236). It's a good flavouring for Victoria sponge (see page 224) or chocolate tart (see page 236), and, apparently, the Swedes bake with it all the time (introduced by the Vikings!). Cyrus has included a Parsee rice pudding recipe on page 233, but my mum's is still the best, I reckon: only milk, sugar, cardamom and rice, no cream, made like a risotto.

Always buy whole cardamom pods, as the flavour will be best. You could remove the seeds from the pod, which is fiddly; or you could bash the pods and seeds together in a mortar or spice grinder, and remove the pod bits if you have the energy or time. Or just use it all – life's too short...

Whenever I had been drinking, I used to chew cardamom seeds so that my dad couldn't smell the alcohol on my breath. He used to smell the cardamom though, and know exactly what I'd been up to!

This is a really simple torte recipe, and if you're really pushed for time you can even buy the sponge base to make it even easier for yourself. The homemade honeycomb may seem a bit scary, but once you've tried it you'll see how easy it is to do.

Tony's

CHOCOLATE & CARDAMOM MOUSSE CAKE WITH HOMEMADE HONEYCOMB

1 Preheat the oven to 180°C/350°F/gas 4. Grease a loose-bottomed 20cm (8in) round cake tin with butter. In a small pan, melt the rest of the butter over a gentle heat and set aside.

2 Pour about 5cm (2in) of water into a separate pan and bring to the boil, then reduce the heat to low. Place the sugar in a metal bowl and sit it on the pan of just-boiled water, checking that the base of the bowl is not touching the water. Break the eggs into the bowl, and with an electric hand mixer beat the mixture over the simmering water for 1–3 minutes, until it becomes pale and frothy. Remove the metal bowl from the heat and continue to beat the mixture for a further 2 minutes while it cools.

3 Gently stir in the vanilla extract and a pinch of salt. With a metal spoon, carefully fold in the sifted flour and cocoa powder. Slowly trickle in the melted butter and continue to combine gently.

4 Pour the mixture into the greased tin and bake for 10–12 minutes or until the centre is firm to the touch. Remove from the oven and cool a little in the tin. Drizzle the whisky over the sponge and set aside to cool completely in the tin.

5 To make the honeycomb, line a 20cm (8in) square cake tin with baking parchment. In a large heavy-based saucepan, heat the golden syrup and sugar together and bring to the boil, then simmer on a low heat for 5–10 minutes. The mixture will bubble and darken to a golden caramel. Mind that the mixture doesn't burn; to test if the caramel is ready, drop a little into some cold water – it should become instantly hard and brittle.

6 Stir in the cardamom and remove the pan from heat. Immediately – but carefully – add the bicarbonate of soda and mix it in; the mixture will instantly foam up significantly, which is why a large pan is needed to prepare the syrup. Pour immediately into the cake tin. Leave to set for

SERVES 6–8

FOR THE GENOISE SPONGE BASE
15g (½oz) unsalted butter, plus extra for greasing
75g (3oz) caster sugar
2 eggs
½ tsp vanilla extract
60g (2½oz) plain flour, sieved
2 tbsp cocoa powder
2 tsp whisky (preferably single malt)
salt

FOR THE HONEYCOMB
2 tbsp golden syrup
100g (4oz) caster sugar
½ tsp ground cardamom (about 12 cardamom pods, seeds finely ground)
1½ tsp bicarbonate of soda

FOR THE CHOCOLATE TORTE
250g (9oz) dark chocolate (70% cocoa solids), finely chopped
430ml (¾ pint) double cream, plus extra to serve (optional)
1 tbsp whisky (preferably single malt)
2–3 tsp ground cardamom (about 50–60 cardamom pods, seeds finely ground)
50g (2oz) caster sugar

Continues overleaf

at least an hour, then break into bite-sized chunks. The honeycomb will stay crisp in a dry, airtight container for a day or two, but will gradually soften over time.

7 To make the chocolate torte, put the chopped chocolate into a large heatproof bowl and set aside. In a bowl, lightly whip together the double cream and whisky until soft peaks form.

8 Pour 200ml (7fl oz) water into a pan, add the ground cardamom and sugar, and bring to the boil, stirring. When just boiling remove from the heat and cool for 30 seconds. Pour through a very fine strainer over the chocolate, stirring continuously to form a smooth glossy mixture. Discard the contents of the strainer.

9 Fold the lightly whipped cream into the chocolate mixture; the mix will start to stiffen. Spoon the mixture over the cold sponge right to the edges of the cake tin, and smooth level. The sponge will have shrunk away from the sides of the tin, so the torte will completely encase the sponge. Cover with clingfilm and chill in the fridge for a few hours, or overnight if possible.

10 To serve, uncover the tin and push out the torte by loosening the base and moving onto a plate. Decorate with honeycomb. Cut into slices (for a smooth, professional finish, use a knife dipped in boiling water). Decorate each slice with more pieces of honeycomb and serve with more double cream, if you like.

This is a mocktail that I created for my daughter's 10th birthday party. They all got dressed up in their glamorous clothes, and we needed a suitably chic drink to set the tone – without any booze, obviously. This definitely does the trick; it's refreshing, great for kids and adults alike, and it looks awesome.

Tony's
SĪNGHS AND THE CĪTY

1 Divide the ice cubes between two highball glasses. Divide the orange juice and pineapple juice between the glasses, then do the same with the grenadine syrup. Garnish with the orange peel and bob a strawberry on the top.

MAKES 2
8–10 ice cubes
200ml (7fl oz) orange juice
200ml (7fl oz) pineapple juice
12.5ml (½fl oz) grenadine syrup
2 strips of orange peel, to garnish
2 small strawberries, to garnish

This moreish drink makes a change from mulled wine, and will warm the cockles of your heart. If you want to avoid becoming too inebriated before a meal, you can bring the rum to the boil before mixing it; this will remove the alcohol while retaining the lovely spiced deepness that this drink brings.

Tony's
SPĪCED
BUTTERED RUM

1 To make the spiced butter, place all the ingredients into a large bowl and beat together until light and fluffy. Transfer the butter mix into a serving bowl and place somewhere cool but not in the fridge; if the fridge is your only cool place, before serving take the butter mix out in time to soften enough to spoon out of the bowl.

2 When you're ready to serve the drink, boil 570ml (1 pint) of water and stir in the sugar to dissolve. Warm the rum in a pan; do not let it get it too hot unless you want to lower the alcohol content or it will start to burn off (this will happen even before the boil). Do take care at this stage too; if the rum gets too hot then there is a risk of it catching fire.

3 Pour the boiled water and sugar mix into the hot rum, then pour into glasses or mugs and pop a cinnamon stick into each one. Let people add their own spiced butter and stir it into the rum with the cinnamon sticks.

SERVES 8-10
80g (3oz) demerara sugar
570ml (1 pint) dark rum
10 cinnamon sticks, for stirring
   the drinks

FOR THE SPICED BUTTER
150g (5oz) unsalted butter,
   softened
80g (3oz) demerara sugar
½ tsp ground cardamom
   (about 12 cardamom pods,
   seeds finely ground)
½ tsp ground nutmeg
1 vanilla pod, use scraped
   seeds only
tiny pinch of ground cloves
   (optional)

SOME SIMPLE SPICE MIXES

Seasonings are part and parcel of cuisine the world over – every type of cooking has its own way of using herbs and spices. Here is a selection of our very favourite spice blends and rubs for you to play with. Try these rubbed or sprinkled onto meat, fish and vegetables before cooking, and experiment with your favourite blends and combinations. Some of them are subtly flavoured, others will blow your head off – but they're all easy to make, and hopefully you will soon realise how simple and fun it is to mix and match to make blends that perfectly satisfy your own personal preferences. These blends will keep in an airtight jar in the fridge for several weeks.

Cyrus
THE RUB-A-DUB ZING

This blend can be used to give a little kick to fish, meat, poultry and much more. Try it sprinkled over some simple sautéed vegetables.

100g (4oz) sea salt
6-8 dried red chillies
2 tsp cumin seeds
1 tbsp coriander seeds
1 tsp black peppercorns

Place all of the ingredients on a baking tray and toast in the oven at 140°C/275°F/gas 1 for 20 minutes. Cool, then grind to a fine powder and store in an airtight jar in the fridge.

Cyrus
TIME FOR SOMETHING A LITTLE MORE ADVENTUROUS

If you can't find any mango powder, look in your supermarket for any other sour fruit powder as a substitute – yuzu powder comes from a dried Japanese citrus fruit and is sometimes more easily available, though be aware that it has a slightly different flavour to mango powder.

100g (4oz) sea salt
6-8 dried red chillies

2 tsp cumin seeds
1 tsp black peppercorns
1 tsp fennel seeds
1 tbsp mango powder

Place all of the ingredients except the mango powder on a baking tray and toast them in the oven at 140°C/275°F/gas 1 for 20 minutes. Cool, then grind into a fine powder and mix with the mango powder. Store in an airtight jar in the fridge.

Cyrus
SHAKE IT ALL ABOUT

This is a simple blend, good for trying on just about anything – though it's particularly useful for roasting chicken, pork or fish. Fill a shaker with this and use it liberally!

1 tbsp garlic powder
1 tbsp chilli powder
2 tbsp ground cumin
1 tbsp ground sea salt
1 tsp caster sugar

Simply put the ingredients in a bowl and mix together thoroughly. Store in an airtight jar in the fridge.

Cyrus

AUNTY PEEGEE'S FAMOUS PARSEE MASALA

Boy, do you have a classic here – this is my family's treasure. An amazing masala, this originates from my mother's cousin (Peegee was not her real name, but this is what I knew her as since childhood. She was like a little angel; she had a very tough life but was always smiling). This recipe takes a little longer, but I'm throwing it into the mix in case you feel adventurous enough to try it. This is adaptable to many things: lamb, pork, poultry, game, beef, etc – just try it and see!

2 tbsp coriander seeds
2 tbsp cumin seeds
6–8 dried red chillies, cut into small chunks
4–5 cardamom pods, bruised with a rolling pin
4–5 cloves
½ nutmeg, grated
1 tbsp fennel seeds
1 tsp black peppercorns
10cm (4in) piece cassia bark,
    broken into small pieces

In a frying pan, gently toast all the ingredients. For best results use a clean tea towel folded several times to make a pad, and use this to push down on the spices, pressing and turning so that they get mixed and toasted. Toast the spices until the mixture becomes darker and you are enveloped with a beautiful aroma around the whole house. Cool and crush in a grinder to a fine powder. The powder will feel a little sticky due to the oil from the nutmeg and cardamom, so keep scraping the sides of the grinder to make sure you catch all of the excess spices.

Cyrus

A FRUITY NUMBER FOR WHEN TIME PERMITS SOME ADVANCE PLANNING

This masala is excellent for meats, especially when cooked with lentils, or for grilling fish or making a salmon gravlax. You can even try marinating fish in this before dipping in batter and frying. Dried fruit peel is easy to make: just remove as much of the white pith as possible from a few strips of peel and simply let the peel rest on a windowsill or near a radiator in winter until it is absolutely dry and crumbles in your hands when pressed. Lime is essential here; lemon is not a suitable substitute.

3 pieces dried satsuma or mandarin orange peel
dried peel of 4 limes
3 tbsp coriander seeds
2 tbsp cumin seeds
2 tbsp fennel seeds
1 tbsp aniseed
2 tsp salt

Place all the ingredients on a baking tray and toast in the oven at 140°C/275°F/gas 1 for 20 minutes. Cool, then grind to a fine powder and store in an airtight jar in the fridge.

Tony

HERBIE GOES BANANAS

A herb-powered blend to use as desired over fish, poultry, salads – anything you can think of! This one will take a few days to make, as you need to allow the salt to help dry out the fresh herbs for an intense flavour.

2 tbsp dill
1 tbsp fresh coriander leaves
1 tbsp fresh parsley leaves
20–25 fresh mint leaves
20–25 fresh basil leaves
200g (7oz) sea salt

Chop all of the herbs together either in a mini food processor or with a knife, and mix with the salt. Place everything on a tray and keep somewhere out of the way in your kitchen. Stir every day until the mixture completely dries out (it will go soft and sticky to begin with, but will eventually dry). Once dried, you can grind to a powder, if you wish.

GLOSSARY

ALLSPICE: Not to be confused with 'mixed spice', which is most commonly used in baking, allspice, also known as Jamaican pepper, is a hard, round berry, which is crushed or ground to release its peppery flavour. The flavour is quite complex – it has notes of citrus, cinnamon and cloves as well as the heat from the pepper – but this makes it a versatile spice, which can be used in both savoury or sweet dishes. It forms the backbone of West Indian cooking.

AMCHOOR: A slightly odd conception, you might think, but no less delicious for it, amchoor is the result of drying unripe mangoes in the sun and then grinding them to a fine powder. As you'd expect, it has a tropical fruit aroma and brings a sweetness to dishes, but it also has a slightly citrusy tartness, which prevents it from being sickly. Amchoor is mainly used in Indian cooking – in chutneys, marinades and curries – but it's usually only added right at the end of cooking in order to preserve its delicate flavour.

ASAFOETIDA: Don't be put off – asafoetida has quite a strong, pungent smell (some say it's dung-like!), but once you've added it to your dish, the ground powder, extracted from a plant in the fennel family, becomes milder and gives your dishes a unique garlicky aroma.

BAY LEAVES: Most commonly used dried (although they are available fresh), bay leaves are added to soups, stocks and stews for the aroma and fragrance they leave behind, and are never actually eaten. In fact, they are hard and have a bitter flavour so it's best to remove them before serving your dish. Bay leaves aren't necessarily the stars of the show – their flavour is subtle – but they work well when used with warmer spices, as they bring out the best in others.

CARDAMOM (GREEN): There are two types of cardamom (see also below). Both are small pods, filled with a cluster of fragrant black seeds. You can use the whole pods (often lightly crushed to extract their flavour) or the seeds in cooking, depending on what recipes call for and how strong a flavour is required. Green cardamom – the more widely available of the two – can be used in savoury and sweet food; you'll find it in Indian fish and meat curries but it's equally as delicious sitting in a dessert, alongside rose water, honey or cinnamon, to provide a sweet, almost perfumed, aroma. (See also page 234.)

CARDAMOM (BLACK): The flavour of black cardamom is different to that of green – it is smoky, which comes from the fact that the pods are dried out over an open fire. Only used in savoury dishes, it is not as easy to come by, nor as commonly used in cooking as green. (See also page 234.)

CAROM: Also know as ajwain, these seeds are pale and look like a lighter version of a cumin seed. They have a strong flavour which is best described as being reminiscent of thyme.

CASSIA BARK: Like cinnamon (see below) cassia bark is the inner bark of a tropical evergreen tree native to India and northern Burma. Although it's harvested in the same way, cassia bark is harder than cinnamon and the sticks have only one layer, rather than the many crumbly layers which make up the more delicate cinnamon sticks. It is also considered to have a stronger flavour than cinnamon and is therefore better suited to flavouring rich meat dishes, where dominant flavours need something that's going to stand up to them. (See also page 128.)

CHILLIES (FRESH): Chillies are a small variety of pepper. They come in different colours (green, red, yellow, orange and black), sizes and heat level, ranging from sweet to fiery hot. Generally the smaller the chilli, the hotter it will be, although even the same kinds of chilli can vary. The membranes that hold the seeds in place contain the bulk of the heat, so you can remove them to lessen the effect. Scotch bonnet and bird's eye chillies are two of the fieriest types of chilli, so if you're not a fan of lots of heat, you should probably substitute these for a milder form. (See also page 102.)

CHILLIES (DRIED/POWDERED): Chillies can be dried to preserve them for longer. Watch out: while you might think the drying process would reduce the heat level, in fact it intensifies the strength and they can become two to ten times hotter because of the shrinkage in size.

Chilli powder is a mix of dried chillies, other spices and salt. If you want to use pure dried chilli powder, go for cayenne pepper. (See also page 102.)

CINNAMON: Cinnamon is the inner bark from several types of tropical tree which, when left to dry, curls up into the familiar quill or stick shapes we buy. It can also be bought already ground, as a powder.

Cinnamon has a slightly sweet, warming aroma that is commonly used in desserts and baking, particularly in the West, or in combination with other spices in Asian, Middle Eastern and North African cooking. (See also page 80.)

CLOVES: The dried flower buds of a tree in the myrtle family, cloves have a sweet but peppery flavour. The buds can be used whole, to gently flavour sauces or stocks or can be studded into hams, onions or fruits. They can also be ground up for an even stronger aroma. Be sure to remove whole cloves before serving and add in moderation as they're quite strong. (See also page 146.)

COCONUT: The coconut available to buy in the UK is actually the stone of a ripe coconut: a hard, brown and hairy shell that needs to be cracked into to reach the creamy, white flesh inside. In the hollow centre of the nut is a clear liquid known as coconut juice or water. This is not to be confused with coconut milk or cream, which are produced by soaking coconut flesh in hot water and straining the liquid. Once strained, a thick cream will rise to the top and the watery milk sits below it. Coconut milk is commonly used in Asian cookery – in curries, sauces, stews but also in desserts.

Desiccated coconut is coconut flesh that has been shredded or flaked then dried to remove as much moisture as possible. There are different types available, mainly according to the size of the flake, but some versions are sweetened too, so you need to make sure you're buying the right type for your recipe. Sweetened desiccated coconut can be used in baking and desserts, but for savoury dishes make sure you're using an unsweetened version.

CORIANDER: The coriander plant produces both a herb and a spice for culinary use. The bright green leaves and stalks of the plant have a fresh, citrussy flavour and given the plant is native to South East Asia, it is most commonly found in dishes from this part of the world. However, it's also used in

South American cooking, where its unique aroma is shown off at its best in uncooked dishes, such as salads and salsas. If you're using coriander in cooked dishes, it's best to add it right at the end to preserve its distinctive flavour.

Coriander seeds are the dried berries from the plant, which are also sold whole or in ground form. Their flavour bears little resemblance to the fresh herb, although you can still detect the citrus notes. As with many spices, you will get the most flavour from the seeds if you dry-fry them before use until their delicate aroma is released. (See also page 192.)

CUMIN: Cumin is a versatile spice, commonly used in cuisines around the world, from India and South East Asia to Morocco and Mexico. The thin and oblong-shaped seeds are best toasted to bring out their nutty, peppery aroma, but you can also buy ground cumin and use it in spice blends or alone. (See also page 34.)

CURRY LEAVES: The curry tree is a member of the citrus family, native to India and Sri Lanka, and the leaves of the tree are most commonly used in dishes from this part of the world and the surrounding region. The leaves have an aromatic, citrussy quality, and are used in much the same way as bay leaves are used in Western cooking. Fresh curry leaves have a short shelf life and will only stay fresh for up to a week, but they freeze well and can be kept for several weeks and cooked from frozen.

FENNEL SEEDS: Like the herb and bulb of the same name, fennel seeds have a delicate aniseed flavour. They marry well with fish but can also be used as one of several spices in a curry or, because of their subtle nature, in desserts.

FENUGREEK SEEDS: These small, oblong, dark brown seeds have a slightly bitter flavour if bitten into raw, but after cooking give off a sweet, almost caramel-like flavour, similar to maple syrup. The seeds will benefit from longer cooking, to ensure you remove the bitterness, so they're often fried in a dry pan before other spices or ingredients are added. Commonly found in Indian cooking, they are generally used in combination with other spices to balance out their sweetness.

FIVE-SPICE POWDER: Although originally Chinese in origin, this mixture of five spices, most commonly star anise, cinnamon, fennel, cloves and Sichuan pepper, is now used throughout Asia. There are of course, variations on the basic recipe, particularly with regard to the quantity of each spice included, but overall the flavour should be a good balance of spicy and sweet, which works particularly well in marinades or as a rub for meat.

GARAM MASALA: Garam masala is a blend of spice powders used in North Indian cooking. The recipe varies according to the region, but typically it contains pepper, cumin, cinnamon, cloves and cardamom. It's traditionally added at the end of cooking, either stirred in, or simply sprinkled over the dish just before it is served. It is available to buy as a ready-made mix, but it's just as simple to make your own.

GARLIC: Part of the same family as leeks and onions, garlic grows as bulbs, made up of cloves encased in a thin, white or purple skin. Most likely you will buy it dried, but there is also a season for fresh (or 'wet' or 'green') garlic (July to the beginning of October), which has a mild flavour and is worth trying if you can get hold of it.

GELATINE: Gelatine is a setting agent made from the bones of animals. It is sold in leaf or powdered form and once rehydrated, it acts to stabilise and thicken desserts, such as custards and jellies. Gelatine leaves just need to be soaked in water for 5 minutes to soften them, then the liquid is squeezed out and they are ready for use. Powdered gelatine is stirred into cold water to make it swell, then dissolved in hot water before use.

GINGER: Ginger is the root of the *Zingiber officinale* plant and comes from the same family as turmeric and cardamom. The knobbly root has a beige skin and a pale yellow flesh and the flavour is slightly sweet, with a kick of heat, which makes it suitable for sweet and savoury dishes. It can also be dried and ground into a powder, which is commonly used in baking – gingerbread being perhaps the best known example – or in spiced dishes, to give them a fiery heat. Be aware that the root and powder are very different and can't be used interchangeably in recipes.

Ginger root can also be preserved in a sweet syrup known as stem ginger, or crystallised and rolled in sugar. Despite its sugary basis, stem ginger does actually work well in savoury dishes as well as sweet – the Chinese often add it to their cooking as an interesting contrast to their salty flavours.

JAGGERY: Jaggery is a type of unrefined sugar, popular in Asian and African cuisine. Sugar cane juice or date palm is boiled down and set into dark blocks to produce a rich, deep flavour, which is similar to caramel.

MACE: Mace is the dried, lacy outer layer of the nutmeg. As such its flavour is very similar to nutmeg although it's more subtle so is used in dishes where nutmeg would be overpowering. It is sold either pre-ground or as blades, which you can grind up yourself. The latter is preferable as the ready-ground mace weakens what is already a very delicate flavour. (See also page 58.)

MANGO POWDER: (see Amchoor)

MUSTARD SEEDS: Depending on the plant they come from, mustard seeds can be white, black or brown, and the flavours all differ subtly. White seeds (which are actually a pale yellow in colour) are the mildest in terms of heat; brown are the ones generally used to make the mustard condiment and are just slightly more pungent than white. Black are the strongest and have a hot, nutty flavour, which is released by toasting the seeds until they pop. These are the most commonly used in Indian cooking.

NUTMEG: The nutmeg tree produces not just one spice but two. The seed of its fruit is coated in a red outer layer, called aril, which when dried produces mace (see above). Beneath this is the nut, which,

after being dried for a month or so, can be broken into to reveal an 'inner nut' – the seed – which is the edible nutmeg we cook with.

Nutmeg is best bought whole rather than ready-ground, where the flavour is quickly lost. Grated freshly, it has a sweet, spicy aroma which is used for sweet and savoury dishes. It's a common ingredient in custard but is also used in sauces, such as béchamel, and curries of all origin. (See also page 58.)

PAPRIKA: Like cayenne pepper (see Chilli, dried/powdered), paprika is a bright red powder made by grinding up dried sweet or hot peppers. The flavour varies from mild to quite hot depending on the type of pepper used, but a recipe will generally state whether you need mild, sweet, or hot paprika. The Spanish also have a 'smoked' version in which the peppers are smoked before being dried and ground.

PECTIN: Pectin is a gelling or thickening agent, which is found naturally in many types of fruit and is commonly used to set jams and jellies. The level of pectin varies according to the fruit: apples have a very high level, for example, while strawberries do not, and if you are using them to make jam they need the addition of lemon juice to boost the pectin level and help set the jam. Pectin can also be bought in liquid or powdered form.

PEPPERCORNS: Peppercorns are used in cooking to add warmth to dishes or to enhance other flavours – try them freshly ground over strawberries, for example, and see how they heighten and accentuate the taste of the fruit. Peppercorns can be used whole, crushed or ground but their potency diminishes very quickly once cracked so to keep fresh they are are best stored whole and used as needed. Similarly, cooking will reduce the strength of flavour so freshly ground pepper is added towards the end of the cooking time or even at the table.

Lightly crushing or cracking peppercorns produces a different result to grinding them. By grinding them you are releasing the full force of their heat, but crushing them is a more gentle alternative, allowing the flavour of the spice to come through, with less of the heat. (See also page 176.)

POMEGRANATE MOLASSES: A sweet, dark, thick syrup made by reducing pomegranate juice and sugar, pomegranate molasses is very common in Middle Eastern cuisine. It works well in sweet and savoury dishes, happily providing a tart contrast to chicken, meat, vegetables or adding a subtle sweetness to salad dressings.

RAPESEED OIL: Made from the bright yellow rape plant that grows abundantly across the UK, rapeseed oil is hailed for its health benefits (it's said to be lower in saturated fat than other oils) as well as for its ability to be heated to very high temperatures without burning or turning rancid. It's therefore a great choice for deep-frying, and if you use the cold-pressed variety, which has a delicate nutty flavour, it's particularly good in salad dressings.

ROSEWATER: Made by steeping rose petals in water, this aromatic flavouring has been used for centuries in Middle Eastern and Indian cooking. Go easy when you add it as it's a concentrated flavour and is very strong, but used with discretion it adds a wonderful dimension to savoury dishes, and partners particularly well with milk and cream to make delicately fragrant desserts.

SAFFRON: Saffron threads are the dried stigma of the saffron crocus. They have a very distinctive aroma and flavour – a little sweet but also slightly bitter which can be overpowering if used in too large a quantity. This means that you only need a little saffron to impart the right balance, which is lucky as it is the world's most expensive spice. The stigmas have to be hand-picked and because there are so few on each flower it takes a huge number of stigmas to make up even a few tens of grams of the spice. As saffron is also often used to colour dishes as well as flavour them, it's a good idea to soak the threads to draw out the colour. You can then strain the liquid and add this to your dish.

SESAME SEEDS: These tiny, flat, oval seeds come in a variety of colours depending on the plant variety, including black, red, brown and, most commonly, a dull white. They have a delicate, nutty flavour and add a delicious crunch to dishes of all sorts – sweet and savoury. They are a dominant flavour in Asian cooking where the seeds are toasted and added to stir-fries or sprinkled over vegetables, but they also crop up in Middle Eastern cooking often, made into tahini paste, or employed in desserts and sweet snacks, such as halva.

STAR ANISE: Shaped like a six- to eight-pointed star, this is an aniseed-flavoured spice which is dominant in Chinese cooking. It's one of the main ingredients in Chinese five-spice powder (see above) and is used whole, simply to infuse dishes, or ground, in baking or as part of a rub or marinade for meat. (See also page 214.)

TAMARIND: The tamarind tree produces a pod containing a sour pulp and many seeds. It is compressed and sold either as pastes or in blocks. Tamarind has a unique sour flavour and is used in cuisines across the world.

TURMERIC: Turmeric is a member of the ginger family, and like its cousin, it comes in fresh root and powdered form. The root can be quite hard to come by and you will most likely have to seek it out in a specialist Asian food shop, but it's worth doing so as the result it produces is very different to the powder.

The powder is known for its ability to give curries their characteristic bright yellow colour as well as an earthy flavour, but turmeric is also lauded for its health benefits and has long been used in Ayurvedic medicine for its anti-inflammatory properties.

TIPS & TECHNIQUES

GRINDING SPICES: Although you might think that buying pre-ground spices is infinitely more convenient and time-saving than toasting then grinding spices yourself, the rewards that grinding bring are worth that extra little effort as the difference in flavour can be astounding. Whole spices should generally be toasted before being ground (see below) and then must be left to cool completely before being ground. You then have essentially two main options. A pestle and mortar is quick, easy and gives you good control over how much or how little your spices are ground; they also have the added bonus of being easy to clean. A coffee or spice grinder (which function in the same way) saves you a lot of muscle power and is good for grinding larger quantities of spices. They're a worthwhile investment if you're going to be grinding spices often to make your own spice blends, and to ensure you get evenly ground powders. Their downside is that they can be a bit of a bore to clean.

STORING SPICES: The longer they are kept the more the flavour and potency of your spices will diminish, particularly ready ground spices. Spices need to be stored in an airtight container in a cool, dark place. While some whole spices, such as cloves, may keep for up to a year if stored correctly, pre-ground spices should be kept for a maximum of six months. This is why it's a good idea to buy your spices in small quantities, ideally from Asian grocers where you can often weigh out the amount you need, and just replace them as necessary, thus minimising the risk they'll go stale. Or grind the whole spices yourself (see above).

TOASTING SPICES: Whole spices are generally toasted (or dry-fried) before being used as this helps to intensify their flavour. You simply put them in a dry pan over a medium heat and toast them until they crackle or pop and release their aroma, stirring occasionally or shaking the pan to prevent burning. Once toasted, spices lose their flavour quickly, so you should always toast them just before you need to use them.

INDEX

ACKNOWLEDGEMENTS

CYRUS For me this book would not have been possible in the timescale within which it was put together without the unfailing support of my wife, Pervin, and our dear friend, Mahrukh Panthaki, both of whom worked tirelessly to make sure that this highly dyslexic man's recipes could be formatted, checked and re-checked, and put into this nightmarish thing called Dropbox! I get so scared that I could drop everything out of sight (as I did last year and lost nearly two books' worth of new, tried-and-tested recipes I was working on). Had it not been for them and their total commitment to making this book so successful, I would still be struggling – what with my work, the business, the kitchen and the programme, plus doing all of the recipes correctly. They pushed the recipes back at me several times until I got them as they were expected to be, and to look like recipes viewed from a layperson's eyes and not those of a chef. So, in short, long live friends and long live wives, without whom husbands like me would remain scatterbrained and disorganised.

TONY Thank you to my wife, Bechan – without her support and encouragement I could never have done what I have. And to my kids, Arrti, Balraj, Seetal and Harpreet. Thank you also to my mum and dad, my granny, my mother-in-law and my father-in-law. Thanks to my brothers and sisters, my cousins, aunties and uncles, and to the lecturer at Telford College and all my head chefs for imparting their wonderful knowledge. And thanks to all the mad, bad chefs I have had the pleasure of rattling a pan with.

ALCHEMY TV Thanks to Tanya Shaw at the BBC for her commitment to the television series behind this beautiful book, along with Tom Edwards and Alison Kirkham. Thanks to the dynamic Fork Off duo Anna Louise Naylor-Leyland and Debbie Pearce. To NL for raising the phoenix. The madly impressive Joe Cottington and Muna Reyal at BBC Books. Alchemy team you rock! Special thanks to Clare Barton, Tim Antill, Caroline Ross-Pirie, Jessica Jones, Tim Hancock, Sue Dulay, Lynette Rees, Shelley Hurley, Jade Hooker, plus Lord Waheed Alli and Charlie Parsons. And of course to Tony and Cyrus for their unique talent and hilarious approach to life.

THE PUBLISHERS We would like to thank Tony, Cyrus and all at Alchemy TV for their hard work, enthusiasm, willingness to help and, perhaps most of all, their ever-cheerful disposition in the face of tight deadlines. Particular thanks go to Nicola Gooch, Caroline Ross-Pirie, Jessica Jones, Tim Hancock, Shelley Hurley, Lynette Rees and Jade Hooker.

NOTES ON THE RECIPES:
- Unless otherwise stated, all eggs are large and all milk is whole.
- Tony prefers to use unsalted butter and Cyrus prefers to use salted butter.
- For fan-assisted ovens, set the temperature 20°C lower than stated in the recipes.
- Check that the fish you purchase has been sustainably sourced.

This book is published to accompany the television series entitled *The Incredible Spice Men*, first broadcast on BBC Two in 2013.

Executive producer for Alchemy TV: Nicola Gooch
Series producers: Caroline Ross-Pirie
and Jessica Jones
Executive Producer for the BBC: Tanya Shaw

10 9 8 7 6 5 4 3

First published in 2013 by BBC Books, an imprint of Ebury Publishing, A Random House Group Company

Copyright © Alchemy TV Limited 2013
Recipes © Cyrus Todiwala and Tony Singh 2013

Photography © Woodlands Books Ltd 2013
Design © Woodlands Books Ltd 2013

The Random House Group Limited Reg. No. 954009

Addresses for companies within the Random House Group can be found at www.randomhouse.co.uk

A CIP catalogue record for this book is available from the British Library.

ISBN: 978 1 849 90578 7

The Random House Group Limited supports the Forest Stewardship Council® (FSC®), the leading international forest-certification organisation. Our books carrying the FSC label are printed on FSC®-certified paper. FSC is the only forest-certification scheme supported by the leading environmental organisations, including Greenpeace. Our paper procurement policy can be found at www.randomhouse.co.uk/environment

Commissioning editor: Muna Reyal
Project editor: Joe Cottington
Copy editor: Marion Moisy
Editor: Susan Fleming
Design: This-Side
Photography: Haarala Hamilton
Food stylist: Aya Nishimura
Food stylist (front cover): Katie Giovanni
Production: Beccy Jones

Colour origination by Altaimage, London
Printed and bound in the UK by Butler Tanner and Dennis Ltd

To buy books by your favourite authors and register for offers visit www.randomhouse.co.uk